PRAISE

PERMANENT REVOLUTION

"At once erudite and intimate, *Permanent Revolution* is a vital set of meditations on difficulty and feminist art. Gail Scott convincingly and beautifully evokes feminism as an ongoing experimental practice: courageous, expansive, and necessary to all."
—Anne Boyer, author of *The Undying*, Winner of the Pulitzer Prize for Nonfiction

"'I can never write the novel I want.' —Gail Scott. In this context, is the sentence a crypt? When does nescience, in the way that word is used by Abraham and Torok, first become a possibility, an analog, a coin, for this other kind of prose, which is to say: 'not a novel' (then)? *Permanent Revolution* is written in the gap between what a novel could have been and what is possible now, and that's a kind of grammar. Reading these essays, I felt the part of me that never writes, but longs to, come back to life for a few moments and/or forever. 'The gap's so great, it's almost comical.' —Gail Scott, who once said that the space between sentences is 'an abyss.' I wrote that down, and thought about it for years afterwards. There was something irreversible, I understood, about what might come next. What will you give up? Who will you never see again? 'That is: where + how in writing?' —Gail Scott."
—Bhanu Kapil

"I can still remember the thrill of first entering the space of Gail Scott's novel, *My Paris*, a diary written all in present participles,

the way I stumbled along the sentences as if around a city. In these essays we get to travel through Scott's thinking through narrative, gender and queer aesthetics, from philosophizing her own experiments in prose to being in conversation with the écriture féminine of friends, from Nicole Brossard's *Mauve Desert* to New Narrative. She also writes through her literary foremothers, from Kathy Acker through the trilogy of the "masturbating French dykes" (ha!) (Irigaray, Cixous, Wittig) to Marguerite Duras. It was Duras's nonfiction I thought about when reading *Permanent Revolution*—profound and poetic, enacting the urgency of literature amidst the emergencies of now."
—Kate Zambreno, author of *Heroines* and *Drifts*

"To experience Gail Scott's *écriture* is to open yourself to 'a wild, titillating, ineffable excess.' Her 'community of sentences' are bodily gestures that we are folded together with, *com-pli-cit*. She gathers the noisy polyglossic surround of her city, 'wilfully fuck[ing]' the caesuras between torn and porous sentences and subjects. What seems at first the limits of articulation with proper listening becomes a beautiful threshold of social space. This book of *essais*, radical tries, charts Scott's writerly formation at the nexus of Québécoise feminist *fiction/theory* and San Francisco queer New Narrative bodily spillage. No one writes quite like Gail Scott, and we all have so much to learn from her untameable work 'at a juncture of politics + excess.'"
—Rachel Zolf, author of *Janey's Arcadia* and *No One's Witness*

PERMANENT REVOLUTION

GAIL SCOTT

PERMANENT

REVOLUTION

Essays

Book*hug Press

TORONTO, 2021

Library and Archives Canada Cataloguing in Publication

Title: Permanent revolution : essays / Gail Scott ; foreword by Zoe Whittall ; afterword by Margaret Christakos.
Other titles: Essays. Selections
Names: Scott, Gail, 1945- author. | Whittall, Zoe, writer of foreword. | Christakos, Margaret, writer of afterword. | Container of (work): Scott, Gail, 1945- Spaces like stairs.
Identifiers: Canadiana (print) 20210129832 | Canadiana (ebook) 20210130210
    ISBN 9781771666824 (softcover) | ISBN 9781771666831 (EPUB)
    ISBN 9781771666848 (PDF) | ISBN 9781771666855 (Kindle)
Subjects: LCSH: Feminism and literature. | LCSH: Prose literature—Authorship.
Classification: LCC PS8587.C623 A6 2021 | DDC C814/.54—dc23

The production of this book was made possible through the generous assistance of the Canada Council for the Arts and the Ontario Arts Council. Book*hug Press also acknowledges the support of the Government of Canada through the Canada Book Fund and the Government of Ontario through the Ontario Book Publishing Tax Credit and the Ontario Book Fund.

Book*hug Press acknowledges that the land on which we operate is the traditional territory of many nations, including the Mississaugas of the Credit, the Anishnabeg, the Chippewa, the Haudenosaunee, and the Wendat peoples. We recognize the enduring presence of many diverse First Nations, Inuit, and Métis peoples and are grateful for the opportunity to meet and work on this territory.

excess   and its containment
is the problem space   par excellence
of late modernity
—Liz Howard

Why do women always have to come off clean?
—Chris Kraus

I'm the gender of Eileen.
—Eileen Myles

TABLE OF CONTENTS

FOREWORD

by Zoe Whittall

"A writer may do as she pleases with her epoch. Except ignore it."

I don't know how to write a foreword, really, let alone a foreword for a book by a writer and thinker I admire as much as Gail Scott, thus I have been putting it off. I've been pulling books off the shelf to study how other writers approach the form. Every once in a while I get up and ride my bike that sits on a stand in my living room, because going outside is ill-advised. It feels like a tangible metaphor, going nowhere as the pandemic rages outside. If I had a bathtub, I'd be in it for several hours a day, soaking in time, just like the narrator of *Heroine*, Scott's most novel-y novel, and the one that changed the way I thought about literature, feminism, queerness, and its intersections. The book that made me feel like I could write a novel that crosses and explodes genre. I love a poet's

1

novel, a plotless novel, one where form and language come before *what happens.*

But I didn't know that until I was assigned *Heroine* in a Women's Literature course at Concordia University in 1995. I attended the class maybe three times because I was too obsessed with going to gay bars, spray-painting the walls of the Plateau with garish hot pink phrases like Pansexual Femmes for Transgender Liberation, watching friends dance at the Chateau-du-Sexe, and planning pro-choice protests. It was more important to be in the blockade for the commemoration of the Dec. 6th massacre than in prose workshop reading a third-rate Hemingway knock-off by a guy named Matt or Brad. I was in university but I didn't know how to write a paper because I'd gone to The New School, an alternative CEGEP where we graded ourselves in Anarchist Theory and watched porn in Feminist Issues class instead of learning how to cite sources or back up our arguments. Even though I dropped the Women's Lit class I devoured *Heroine* over and over in my small, cold room on the Plateau, amazed at what writing could be. I remember thinking, *I could do this.* This is an open possibility, this is poetry and theory and language, *and* it's political. This is the sentence, the word. We called everything postmodern back then, but this really was it. I'd begun to read Kathy Acker and Eileen Myles, Gary Indiana and Dennis Cooper, and the surge of queer writing coming out of small presses like Semiotexte and Soft Skull in the United States. In Montreal it felt like everything avant-garde and boundary pushing was coming from New York and San Francisco. *Heroine* opened me up to New Narrative in my home province, to écriture-au-féminin, and the province I thought was apart from anything experimental or cutting edge in the arts was suddenly its epicentre. Scott's work represented a world where women, queers, and outsiders could participate in the academy and be intellectuals, the opposite of what I was being taught in my creative writing workshops at Concordia, where anything political went against the purity of the solo, isolated, and idealised artist, and where queer and feminist content was dismissed as less than, nothing close to intellectually rigorous.

For those of us who devour Scott's work, the essays in *Permanent Revolution* answer the question, What has she been thinking about art, new and difficult writing, narrative and its breaking points, community, and revolution, for the last twenty years? For those who are new to Scott's work, the collection will serve as an excellent introduction to an iconic thinker in the field of the feminist and queer avant-garde. Scott discusses the history of the New Narrative movement and its current iterations, looking at both its influence and its evolution and newest practitioners. Best of all, like everything she writes, the book invents the form as it goes, and asks the reader to sink into her unique prosody and mesmerizing sentences.

Zoe Whittall
Toronto, 2021

PREFACE

Permanent Revolution[1] traces my trajectory of prose experiment to the present, relating the act of writing to ongoing social upheaval. The essays are in conversation with English-language experimental prose across the continent, notably in the field of queer New Narrative. This book contains a foreshortened re-creation of *Spaces Like Stairs*, a personal record of the writing-in-the-feminine movement in 1980s Québec.

The term *Permanent Revolution* has its roots in Marxism; I have gleaned from it what I want for purposes of foregrounding prose experiment as crucial to those who identify as women; +, by extension, to proximate others on the ever widening scale of gender distribution. To recognize that gender minorities are—as are other diverse minorities—in a *permanent* state of emergency as concerns life + the expression of it is necessarily to reshape how we narrate as a species. A species that thinks, at least in part, back through our mothers. A living community is also a community of sentences, signing, in particular, our relationship to female ancestors.

There is nothing that sets the scene better for this than Mina Loy's feminist manifesto with its almost scornful call-out to women: *"Is that all you want?"* Rising in the professions, she warns, is not enough! *"NO scratching on the surface of the rubbish heap of tradition will bring about **Reform**, the only method is **Absolute Demolition**."* I don't have to agree with everything in that manifesto to see that Loy is on the right track in calling for fundamental change in the entire set of systems/institutions that impact us.

If the focus in my work was, up to the early 90s, an exploration of the question of the feminine in writing, the new + recast essays featured here are concerned with diverse notions of 'Fe-male.' They are a modest evolutionary snapshot of various approaches + concerns—notably class—in the writing of my later novels, work that was accompanied by my travelling the continent in search of other experimental prose writers working in English.

I am finalizing the collection in a dire period of pandemic, climate calamity, the continued police assassination of Black + Indigenous peoples, coupled with ongoing indifference regarding missing + murdered Indigenous women.

A writer must do as she can with her epoch. Rage accumulates.

Gail Scott
Montréal, 2021

THE SMELL

OF FISH

//

EXCESS + THE FEMININE

As if a genie escaping the bottle, a wild, titillating, ineffable excess seeps from certain writing + visual art by women. It rustles mid the blossoms, lacy garlands, + round geometries of early 20th century Swedish Hilma af Klint's paintings. It draws me into the strangely everyday magnetism of Agnes Varda films. It glimmers between the phrases of the zanily accurate women in Jane Bowles' prose. It glitters from somewhere beyond the starry high street wires of Clarice Lispector's Brazilian tales. It lurks in the torqued + fractured terrain of Sheila Watson's prose, radiates off lesbians in a bar in Nicole Brossard's *Picture Theory*. But why—if excess defines the limit where all good art expresses—must one speak in particular of excess-in-the-feminine? Does code open here to what has not been said or is said but cannot yet be read; some indicible vibration signalling as unauthorized meaning, "a meaning to come, impossible," wrote Kristeva. And can we even term that elixir as feminine in an era when gender binary seems passé as concept?

Standing in the Guggenheim, looking at Hilma af Klint's largest paintings, all pastels, loops, curlicues, I thought: déjà vu, this overwrought, almost clichéd, femininity. Gazing harder, I, with my friend, + a whole row of viewers, were leaning bodies more + more forward, as if magnetized by something happening there, something almost religious, or cabalistic in that palette of pinks, lavenders, peaches, baby blues, with cursive scripted Swedish woven into the pretty round surfaces. We were drawn by what, precisely? *By the freshness,* offering a critic, *of symbolic associations with feminine iconography* [there was no elucidation regarding the meaning of 'feminine iconography']. Af Klint herself, who has just, a mere century later, been anointed the first Western abstract artist, knew these works were before their time, decreeing they not be shown till well after her death. Meanwhile, she paraded as respected landscape artist while quietly making extensive notes, cataloguing, designing a temple, no less, to house her real work. Which temple's three-level conical structure bore an eerie resemblance to the coiled shell of the Guggenheim, its winding corridor on which we spiralling our way upward. Excited. Then uneasy. The exhibition's curated insistence on af Klint's 'spiritualism' [her women's group of paranormal explorers] seemed to be obfuscating the brash—almost promiscuous—geometries hanging there, emanating something akin to an unusual perfume, some signal not yet named. One *could* call it 'feminine'. But again, why say 'feminine' for this work? Unless one says 'masculine' for Kandinsky's.

The West Village bistro's a four-storey, dark-panelled, pre–Civil War brick structure. You see riverboat men, perhaps coming in after work on the nearby Hudson. The door opening with a rush of salt sea air—in those less polluted days more tangy. And Walt Whitman sitting—maybe cruising—there among them. One can imagine such seductions, unspoken, wafting from between the lines of certain Whitman poems. But it is March 2019 + the poet Marjorie Welish is sitting opposite. Also a visual artist, her poetry, for me, lies somewhere between disjunct text + signage. Lines like

Never did I receive your/Public lettering[1]

emitting a startling intensity from the spaces between words/lines on the page. You are confessing to her your initial impatience with af Klint's tender yet troubling surfaces, their slow release, in the viewing, of some brash female excess. If, indeed, whatever issues from them *might* reference the 'feminine'? Marjorie, also a superb art critic, is laughing, handing you two notebooks. One tiny, one larger. "I hope you give it to them," she teases.

What 'it' is, for me, is that which is not said, is mostly not described, that which seeps from the margins of the term + seems, of little consequence to the centre. It calls up the late Caribbean writer Édouard Glissant, saying as regards the creolization of language, that as the ideological discursive centre congeals, minority tongues get displaced to the periphery. They become creolized, but the dominant language is also unconsciously altered in the process. It is tempting to apply this notion in different degrees, + sometimes overlapping contexts, to what may be potentially coded female. Especially since, Glissant continues, what has been lost in the scramble is the *content of oral tradition*.[2] He is speaking of something hidden deep in memory, tonal, a-syntactic. For purposes of recovering this elixir, he is clear that it takes not description but deep language excavation to reconnoitre the fundaments of what has grown discontinuous, even schizophrenic, under the weight of the historic.

Might this reconnoitring process in any way be akin to af Klint's paranormal research, her group of women around a Ouija board, receiving messages from a so-called other world? Or Jane Bowles, sitting ecstatic in the Tangiers grain market, fascinated by lover Cherifa's knowledge of magic? Or Sheila Watson, gone silent to burnish the career of her poet husband, having written stories with titles like "My Brother's Name Is Oedipus." Or surrealist Leonora Carrington tripping through madness, imagining a paradise called "Down Below" where people live *very happily. To reach that paradise it was necessary to resort to mysterious means which I believed were the divination of the Whole Truth.*[3] A radical religious upbringing on one hand, + my grandfather's fortune-telling in the backroom of his small-town jewellery shop, fostered in me a confidence in the value of the suppressed or hidden, thus the desire to transgress the normal. I joined a left-wing group's arty surrealist phalange, spending hours weekly researching, via automatic writing + exquisite corpses, the illusive codes of what they called objective chance. I knew there was something else.

I walk on. My special glasses see, in the window of a photo store, a picture of a girl and a soldier holding hands under a big tree. But the soldier is X'd out and underneath is written: Ecartez le soldat. In the next picture the soldier is effectivement écarté. There's just the girl. What I like is the anti-militarism of the sequence (for there's revolt in Portugal). Also, the refusal to acknowledge the soldier's tragedy. Surrealism hates nostalgia, a key ingredient of war. (But where are you, my love, this minute? And why are you so angry?) Never mind that. I have to be prepared to take what comes. Letting each passing minute bear its fruit. A chance meeting of two lovers, as of two images in a poem, produces the greatest spark. Like André Breton who by chance met Nadja and took her as his génie libre. The better to see the world through the vision of her madness. Then he wrote a great novel. Except I don't like the way he used her. Oh, I'll have to test the guys in my surrealist group on the women's issue.

"Speaking of anomalies," I say (later, as we're sitting around the table in their apartment on St-Denis), "speaking of anomalies, what if you're going along a sunny street. And suddenly from a dark alley this jewelled hand comes out. In a black glove. And pulls you in. Then it's uh rape?"

Looking at me with his red-spotted face (he has some nervous disease) and round John Lennon spectacles, R says, really embarrassed: "A person should probably know self-defence."[4]

In the tiny red notebook from Marjorie I write passwords. Those often lost, forgotten, misremembered perpetrators of my everyday chaos. But on the minuscule first page, I must have noted at lunch [ginger squash soup/red wine]: *Mesmerisms. Gertrude Stein.* If various last-century artists, especially the Surrealists, used the preternatural to free themselves from restrictive reasoning, Stein was proudly derisive of the automatic writing experiments in her student days at Harvard. Yet she was fascinated by what those exercises revealed of the 'bottom nature' of the human personality—especially in terms of cyclical patterns of speech. Indeed, Stein loved to commingle, in her writing, so-called primitive + complex mental processes, allowing her sentences to be wilfully fucked by soldier argot, French grammar, Cubist constructions, or plain whimsy. So many portraits of women [Ida, Alice, the Good Anna] project figures—sometimes problematic, as were her politics—but brilliantly at the edge of normal parameters of 'female.' 'Fe-male' here more apt than feminine. Stein, in fact, more butch than femme—seeming to question if the lesbian was a woman at all.

A house in Outremont, late 80s [anti-feminism on the rise], our *Théorie, un dimanche* group gathers around Nicole's elegant dining table. One is musing whether the lesbian a woman. Another saying that, as far as the gender spectrum, she feels relatively feminine—but sans the least desire for male attention. It takes the late great Louky Bersianik to keep us focused on language, noting that 'le féminin' is a noun of the *masculine* gender, rendering an essentializing interpretation of 'le féminin' questionable. As we moved toward the 90s, the cool gender placeholder was increasingly 'queer' in progressive milieus. So subjectivity was performance, a costume, having to do with repetition *very often with the repetition of oppressive and painful gender norms to force them to resignify.*[5] The more camp, the more outrageous, the more the work grew politically + aesthetically effective. New York writer Eileen Myles has famously declared: *I'm the gender of Eileen.*

//

Late August 2020: Montréal militants have knocked over the statue of John A. Macdonald on account of his fostering the residential school system for First Nations children. Prime Minister Trudeau is disappointed. It is uncivilized to cancel history. How does this parse with continuous mention of Truth + Reconciliation + repeated *verbal* acknowledgement of unceded territories at, say, literary gatherings? With nary a consequential discussion of the material issue of vast occupied territories. Without which progress is obstructed. The oft-repeated conundrum for feminists who write: acknowledging white imperialism by working to dismantle a subject formed by the egocentric West—while resisting gender-based erasure. This is a formal issue—but surely it cannot be perfected in solitude. Glissant suggested: whether one speaks one language or many, what we speak is haunted by history. The remarkable young Indigenous writing emerging in recent years is exemplary: Liz Howard, Jordan Abel, Billy-Ray Belcourt, all winners of the prestigious Griffin, all exploring layers of identitary issues by foregrounding First Nations knowledge— deploying deeply haunting language—both in confrontation, + in conjunction with science, computer technology, + philosophy.

Last summer in Paris—my lucky pre-pandemic 2019 summer!— conjures a romanticized association with the film *Last Year at Marienbad*: that strange woman of erased history walking over black and white tiles. Indeed, last summer in Paris, I met a group of intriguing young women, practising a life of making art, fervently distancing from dominant discourse + its practices. Living on the margin [+ of course they were beautiful], doing nothing but their art; writing, printing, designing, publishing, preparing *'gouine'* performance interventions for political events + demonstrations. One *Parisienne* offers me two texts: the Édouard Glissant interview quoted here. And a work about the troubadours in which poet Jacques Roubaud, of Oulipo fame, is saying that writing prose began as explanation, interpretation, or biographic comment on the *canzo* [chansons/love songs] of the troubadors, in order to thicken the lyric *present* of the amorous troubador. The implication being that prose is rooted in purpose, notably for the sake of establishing history/sense of tradition, + by extension, the establishment of authority, concomitant with nation-building requirements in that far-off era of new consolidating nation states.[6] But must prose be merely the *razo*, the interpretive frame, the ring band holding the beautiful diamond of the poem at its centre? Of course, the prose I dream of requires a more adventurous spirit from the reader— + the author. The formalist prose writer + critic Viktor Shklovsky, though speaking, early post–Russian Revolution, far from our era of reading-as-scanning, admitted that reading his prose could be *long and laborious.* [And here again are af Klint's paintings, obliging one to pause, until the more one looks, the more one perceives.] *The technique of art is to make objects unfamiliar, to make forms difficult, to increase the difficulty and length of perception because the process of perception is an aesthetic end in itself and must be prolonged. Art is a way of experiencing the artfulness of an object: the object is not important...*[7] In this era of hyper-rapid communication, is this to be seeming hopelessly utopian?

If af Klint envisioned her painting inhabiting a spiralled environment, its curves, loops, curlicues, spacy weird balloon-like shapes not quite rubbing against each other mirror for me the device of enjambment in poetry. I am wryly envious of the sense of the almost religious superiority some attach to the poetry form. But I take as a sign of our times that many poets are going over to prose—could this imply that whatever faint suggestion of narrative lurks in the space of enjambment in some eras calls for sentences? I like to think the best prose combines, via formal inquiry, the best aspects of both poetry + prose, aesthetic + non-aesthetic. Leaving room for the unsaid: a heterodox movement between both the time + space of narrative + of the process of inscription that scatters the subject across the environment.

Stretched on friend R's Brooklyn sofa, days after the af Klint exhibition, I am still wondering if that elixir, that strangeness seeping from af Klint's genial, belatedly crowned work, may aptly be termed 'feminine?' R is driving across the desert from Arizona to California to visit her mother—that is, over the imaginary terrain of Nicole Brossard's *Mauve Desert*. Where, in some motel or trailer, Brossard's lesbian family is living. And in another motel-room-pocket in the middle of the novel lies *l'homme longue*, stretched out on a bed. He has something to do with the atomic bomb. Strangely, these few pages about a man, written by one who mostly writes about lesbians—beautiful, female, + yes, somewhat feminine lesbians—these pages, framed in the gaze of her novel, are among Nicole's most formally compelling prose.

I would also like to mention a certain 'queer' representation—but not what is meant by the term in French or English—in the prose of 2-spirit author Joshua Whitehead. If one wants to think of art as permanent revolution, it can't be single-issue anything. And Joshua Whitehead's *Jonny Appleseed*, a novel I last winter read 3 times in a row, is exemplary in gathering the intersectional layers, juxtaposing two tales intertwining in the narration. In one, Jonny is living in Winnipeg, trying to survive by virtual hustling, an urban narrative that is juxtaposed on their return to life back on the rez with their beloved mother + grandmother. The latter site being one of a whole social structure + language + living in a community, a set of values that John A. Macdonald + white settler culture still seek via ignorance + indifference to suppress. Poet Liz Howard also brilliantly entwines Indigenous culture + European in her work:

the women of bitumen looked over tailing ponds
like a cloud-rack of a tempest
rushed the pale canoes of wings and thunder
to kill the wilderness in the child[8]

But here is that perfume again, that perfume of the hidden I cannot put into my English words. I gather about me some favourites, basking in the elixir that seeps from the crevices of their creations. In addition to Joshua Whitehead, Liz Howard, Lisa Robertson: *I'll be lost, then, if reading is dark. In the forest, in the hotel or wherever.*[9] Jane Bowles whose character Harriet, whose equally old-maid sister has followed her to "Camp Cataract," ruining her vacation. A master of the suppressed aside, Bowles' protagonist declares: "*I don't fight with Sadie… I wouldn't dream of fighting like a common fishwife. Everything that goes on between us goes on under-cover….*"[10] Another favourite: Black U.S. writer Renee Gladman, whose circular sentencing raises *témoinage* to the heights of poetic expression: *Since noon, there has been a group of whites marching along the edge of the park, cheering for the grass to be cut. They worry that we are doing drugs in the weeds—that the colored people are. Because I'm lying in the grass, representing that scenario, the noise is loudest around me….*[11] And Clarice Lispector, whose last heroine is nobody, a woman utterly insignificant inside + out, lying dying in the gutter after being knocked down by a snazzy yellow convertible, becoming, in some estranging transformation, suddenly relevant, alive, with a candle someone has placed by her side. Agnes Varda's films, so much, on the surface, about the ultra-ordinary everyday, yet, having entered the cinema, quite unhappy, I emerge from *Visages/Villages* feeling I have been in an interactive experience, loved, nurtured. Without understanding what essence, in the exchange between us, derailed my despondence. An anecdote: a poet I know was doing a reading somewhere in the North to a captive classroom group of teenagers. In an oblique reference to lesbian sex, she mentions the smell of fish. Several dozy heads go up.

Some of us like the smell of fish very much.

THE ATTACK OF DIFFICULT
~~WOMEN~~ PROSE

Like old snake-oil purveyors, writers have to travel. To display
their wares before the shelf life expires [to be female's to be well-
versed in the irony of that!]. Infinite, over centuries, have been the
efforts of women on the move to release their particular geni(us)
from the bottle. Kept plugged, she's perfume. Uncorked, fusty.
Indecipherable. "Nothing happens in this novel!" "Maybe she
would make a better poet." Even New York writer Lynne Tillman,
whose prose is sister to that of Jane Bowles, cites difficulty in deciphering how Bowles *entraps dreams, fantasies, waking life, conscious
and unconscious thoughts in one sentence. I remain,* she writes, *surprised,
even dumbfounded, by how she does it.*[1] One could ask of so many
female writers for at least a century...: WHY

*Sentences. Running sideways. Back. Forth. Beginning one way.
Turning, unexpectedly. Like insects in a glass. Or people rushing
round her bench in the airport. Woman sniffs profusely. "Take care*

of Mommy." Daddy telling worried boy toddler. Lesbian sitting. Trying to hide her longing. Entire airport echoing within. The lover gone. The space between them. Mobile.

Have you noticed, between sentences, you can move the spaces?

Choosing, driving back to town, road under misty trees under the bank of the city. Passing favourite building in Chinatown. BREATHE. *Red + white-checked front. High rotting bay windows. Covered with pigeon shit. Two skinny ragged youth. Walking in front. One raises bandaged arm. The sentence as gesture.*

Have you noticed you can move the periods?

She parks in the heat. Enters a room. Still white in morning light. What ruins. Half-empty wine glasses. A bottle marked Barefoot. Rounder goblets with sticky brandy traces. Colliding. Over-charged with meaning. Re-membered silhouette. On knees. Arched back and pretty raised hand. Fingers bent. And plunging— Did the neighbours hear? Did they feel disgust?

A sentence may (even) be constituted as a figure of synthesis in violation of syntax [old Oxford dictionary]: *Obs written after.*

//

A word about the DIFFICULT: In the alchemy between art + estrangement, notably in times of left + right populisms, failure to mirror the familiar brands the innovative prose writer as *not* blue ribbon. If under the sway of a desire to reach the widest audience, a tendency to bend toward the obvious may result in…*the flaw, the error of first sight* [which] *is to see, and not to notice the invisible.*[2] Contiguously, so-called 'difficult' work may be said too feminist of persuasion, or disturbingly transgender, or slapped with any other diverse minority identitary tag, + not assessed for its art. A critic in a prestigious Canadian literary journal, puzzling over the lack of active verbs in my millennial novel, *My Paris*, written almost entirely in present-participle phrases, concluded—and this was not intended unkindly—that my novel must be a case of lesbian aesthetics.

It was with Beckett, I travelled. Dragging my battered steamer trunk behind. Full of stacked notes, marked reading copies of his + lesser-known avant-garde novels. Not to mention facial care treatments, feminine hygiene products. A redingote! The trunk becoming plastered, over time, with identifying stickers: FEMINIST, LESBIAN, LEFT-WING, EXPERIMENTAL, ANGLO-QUÉBÉCOISE. Beckett, ambling along beside, bearing underarm a simple handcrafted leather case stamped WRITER. Getting off trains, I glanced back to see his case was not forgotten. Pandering to ancient catechisms of protecting masculine freedom to be charmingly distracted. Immoderately seduced by his penchant for resisting 'sense,' on which literary barristers have heaped so much respect. *Cou-rage*, says a friend [etymology (Fr.): *heart-anger*]. "Think of it as noise. As I do with Adorno." She stands as if on stage. Bright magenta lipstick. Skirt just above knees. Hair blowing cinematically. She/*Anaïs walks to the window, flings it wide remembering a similar gesture made by Elizabeth Taylor and Alice B. Toklas*.... This *action throws resentment to the wind...* assuring that *the pleasure of the moment is hers*.[3]

In what utopia is Anaïs's gesture in the aperture of the enclosure a trope for women wanting to *approach, intuit, touch, to seize upon the* *inextricable of the world?*4 Is not Anaïs's gesture, within the portal, followed by double-work [we are also familiar with the irony of that]? *...first she writes then she impresses the writing on paper.* All the while restraining her energetic spirit *from bolting up to whoever's apartment as she does not want energy to be mistaken for desperation.*5 Her self-published letters, commodious in their way of explaining women to men, wrought in language the tender male of the species finds neither emasculating nor unreasonable. One could also ask: Is her gesture—one could say strategy—leashed to impulses learned in the figurative enclosure, an impediment or ticket to freedom? And once released, once beyond the gate, will she, Anaïs, be full participant in public discourse?

I sit on the edge of my hotel bed. Fe-male, but not skirtable enough to rustle, fashionably bespectacled, impeccably professional [a mite flirtatious], in the folds of the codex. Though why should a woman not use every wile in her repertory to achieve her considerable ambitions? My concern: One's choice of sociability may risk impacting creative outcome. But why then travel with the likes of Beckett? Is my *heart-anger*, if bedazzled by his genius, not risking hesitating to move forward at the edge of a precipice? *If the line simply continues without being crossbred with the non-esthetic fact, nothing is ever created.*6 I am taking the non-aesthetic fact to mean expression of the entire range of exclusion: Gender [all of them]. Race [for those not people of colour, the task is, I believe, to participate in a critical construction of whiteness]. Class [always class].

...they are burning coal down the road to power this light
*I want my poem to be worth the heart of a mountain*7

Walking, nights in my redingote, I am fiction: a lesbian. To a voice in the dark querying what males most need to change, I shout *the gaze*. Yet, knowing full well that *to be Fe-male*'s to be a-part of it. Sometimes, I wonder if 'she' in-the-feminine is not akin to Marx's Specter—that mysterious aura that gleams off + heightens value of consumable objects on way to market? Attention, warned Marx, the aura is not an essence; it is *a secret that is all the more secret in that no substantial essence hides behind it*.... The effect is born of social relation.... And Marx goes on to say this *Socius* binds *on the one hand men to each other.*[8] On the other hand [I intervene], it attempts to bind me to the agents of custom.....................HA!

It STINKS, my old steamer trunk. When I open + let fly yellowed scraps attempting to speak the unspoken, mixed with recipes, dark underwear, old makeup, accoutrements to prevent odour, conceal shameful body [mis]-function [increasing with age]. I laugh, though, like my sisters, I am vascillating between full, proud expression of *heart-anger* +incommodious outbursts that diminish, in the eyes of many, one's literary efforts. We who are by no means homogenous, wherever we are on the gender spectrum, are various in our choice of strategies, as we strive to be eternally *young before the world*. Craving...that *youth,* [its] *capacity to feel all the world's flows mixing together in a completely unexpected and completely inextricable way. Utopia is the force of feeling this*....[9] Hence, my question for master Beckett: how, for instance, to stick 3 heads in 3 vases, fill speaking mouths with love-betrayal, the stuff of women's romance fiction. And win the Nobel:

W1: till all dark   then all well   for the time   but it will come
W2: poor thing   a shade gone   just a shade   in the head
M: all as if   never been   it will come   *Hiccup.* Pardon.
W1: the time will come   the thing is   there you'll see it
W2: *Laugh*.... just a shade   but I doubt it
M: no sense in this   oh I know   none the less[10]

His hubris: to take the simplest of words between a man + his competing women lovers; to make a lattice of them, a pattern, contrapuntal, setting in relief that site where abstraction + iterative custom meet. The efficiency of the gesture, almost shocking. Actress Juliet Stevenson, who initially found his work pretentious, abstruse…, to be declaring: *It's interesting, Beckett so often wants to contain women. So…it was a complete revelation: to come inside the material, and explore it and inhabit it. And I realised he really is a genius.*[11]

Another word about DIFFICULT: For me, the formal dispersal of the writing subject over an accidented terrain is what signs adventurous prose. The divets in the narrative arc thus rendering the novel or story relatively subject to the aleatories of language, + diminishing definitive author/narrator/character divisions, in the way of poetry. But not quite poetry, inasmuch as one has to also deal with the forward impulse of sentence movement toward that definitive stop, the period. But the call for quick answers in the face of contemporaneous calamity may leave experimentalists, already struggling against the decline of teaching of poetry in the academy, deep in the smog. Who needs the defamiliar in this pandemic winter, spring, summer, fall, when the facts are already estranging in themselves? NO ONE HAS SEEN ANYTHING LIKE THIS BEFORE.

The answer is that many of us are not, in the context of our everyday, cast in a mold that reproduces the psychology of what is generally considered 'the familiar'. Perhaps, also, there is a stubborn refusal of the déjà vu. Dithyrambic reviews of certain novels that are larded with sentiment, lauding what seems so obvious, so always already said, have sometimes made me want to shout: *Take your thumb out of your mouth.* Marguerite Duras, more elegantly, was of the opinion that there are often narratives but very seldom writing: And Charles Bernstein, more empathetic: *...I see the fate of all of us as related to a lack of judgment, a lack of cultural and intellectual commitment, on the part of the PWC*[12]—[publications with wide circulation].

I long for a time when writers wore upstart intellectual performance as a badge of honour. There is, in the CBC archives, a hilarious 1977 interview with young Margaret Atwood suggesting on national TV that interviewer Hana Gartner would be better off reading Harlequin romances. This in response to Gartner's declaring she cannot empathize with Atwood's depressing stories. Atwood is no difficult writer but she is a Canadian literary figure who has not hesitated to don the mantle of bitch when the situation required. When will more of us return to speaking up? *And in whose interest is it that we do not?*

//

RUSSIAN Viktor Shklovsky's early post-revolutionary Formalist novel *Zoo* was written in exile in Berlin, where he fled from a Communist regime's growing censure + surveillance. A little more than half a century later, Atwood's *The Handmaid's Tale* recounted extreme patriarchal suppression + constraint of women for reproductive purposes. It coincided with a gathering concern that we were once more entering a society of surveillance in Capitalist regimes. Not long after that, in a *New Yorker* cartoon: A man, sun hat pulled down, expectant look of pleasure on face, beach grass blowing in a way that signifies New England. But no sooner had he settled on his lawn chair + opened the precious object, his book, than a soldier approached, informing the man that... *We don't consider Dostoevsky summer reading. You'll have to come with us.* This hints at the degree to which American liberals were already concerned prior to 9/11 + the invocation of the Homeland Security Act, with the question of surveillance. What the cartoon implied is all the more relevant today: i.e., 1) Dostoevsky, trope for the literary, is still a danger from which citizens may need protection. 2) An inference, with the arrival of the soldier, whose presence seems a warning to the guilty subversive in each of us, that to like Dostoevsky [i.e., the literary] might be a cover, an auto-repressive gesture; the man on the beach might really be hankering to read something even more seditious. The soldier, being both less + more substantial than he appears = champion of the obvious, as determined by some moody overload of information keeping public opinion too frantic to concentrate on anything more complex. *We're too tired to make love... We need to overthrow the government... We're too tired to overthrow the government....*[13] The bottom-line mentality of the soldier at once balloons up into a reminder that public opinion is...US. We who are too exhausted to be troubled, to make an effort.

The 'dead author [Dostoevsky]' pun offers one more fusty portal. In this epoch of 'virtual' extension of 'self' via an endless stream of information, there have been continuous claims that Author as Arbitrator of the relation between language + thinking is dead. Musty. Past expiry date. Literary efforts to split, flay, mock, deconstruct + reconstruct thought, from Dada onward, seem to preclude this moment when people, materially dispersed by politics + economics, + increasingly uncertain of origins, are meant to be in search of comforting bromides.

But, as the younger generations are teaching us, new global circumstance is ultimately less about free expression of the bounded individual, than it is about finding a balance between independence/inter-independence of being. To wit: behind society's notion of the 'feminine' as commodious, seductive, there lurks—until she begins to crack the glass that contains her—a question that needs an answer. A question deeply embedded in what is meant by balance of power in the Polis.

SOFT THINGS,
HARD THINGS

*But I can't close without mentioning the interval between the
appearance of* Theory, A Sunday *in French and its appearance in
English. (Fr. 1988/Eng. 2013)*

As this reminds me of a screechy sound, Eeeeeeeegleeesh?
It's The Obituary's *last word and only cry. It comes from the figure
of a laughing little girl, of "French. Québécois. Greek. Indigenous.
Also Caucasian-American ancestors." As a way to end a work it
is excessive, skeptical, funny, unsettling like* The Obituary *itself.
Eeeeeeeegleeesh?*

Yeah, that noise tells me it's time to go pull some weeds.
—Carla Harryman, on *The Obituary*[1]

My tangled literary web is motile, a map of the continent. Dynamic with affections + [mostly suppressed] conflict. As regards the country called America [I also live in America but in a country not called America], I possess, by definition, a North reticence re South culture's truculent rodomontades—next our tendency toward circuitous fashion of address, said hypocrisy by some. To wit: being specialists of pro-climate rhetoric, we are yet munificently hosting with tax dollars, subventions, exemptions, rock-bottom royalties from climate-retrogressive oil-sands purveyors. Or is our circuitry of discourse in this land, stolen from others, in this nation, with its many back loops, twists, deviations from the centre, just still in search of a collective public discourse? One could, with such preoccupations, write a Russian novel:

X, a Californian, sitting in a summer dre-e-ess, marvelling the Vancouver day still warm enough for that. Y, just in from Montréal, sits, stinging, furious, beside. Still reeling from stumbling on that girl tied to a bed last night in a Plateau Mont-Royal flat. Her face sets disconsolate, scornful, on the Canadian poet making introductory remarks to the conference of self-described avant writers. He, skinny, bearded, eagerly hoisting several [mostly male] US cohorts up the 'new poetics' staff.[2] True, Y agrees we must be dismantling lyric self-expression in favour of some more defamiliarizing or conceptual method. Is she not a revolutionary on every front? Only why can't these new poetic men grasp that to erase the speaking subject ENTIRELY risks erasing a range of minority subjectivities already diminished in the canon?

She tosses curls that half conceal a mediocre profile. Dander rising by the minute, now determining an Anglo-Canadian feminist's paper is cursory to point of superficial, being too dependent on brief translated excerpts from some French feminist anthology. Has not her group in Montréal been reading all of these authors' works in the original French—*Kristeva, Cixous, + so many others, in their entirety? A photo of the Vancouver conference shows several hairy-faced young men + cheerful smiling women poets, against some kind of lush Vancouver setting. The tension is palpable. X, a rare US Language Poet also passionately feminist, is at the end of a row. Thoughtful, the sole woman not smiling, her curls flaring to her shoulders, wearing that summer dre-e-ess in the way only a woman of warmer climes can. Notwithstanding Y's pain, this is a very romantic moment.*

Russian literature is devoted to the description of unsuccessful love affairs.

Our schools make us. But we make them, too, shards, tendencies, a little knee-bending to please whatever cohort, for one must have love somewhere, subsumed—*IF there is writing*—in the woof + wharf of a trajectory. Having taken the aleatory for freedom, having pasted *EXPERIMENTAL* over the identitary tags on my travelling accoutrements, I, after a trip to San Francisco, begin eliding experimental with queer as per the local New Narrative writers. Indeed, the shape-shifting identitary + art possibilities of 'queer' felt airier in that moment of severely backlashed 90s feminism.

Sure enough. The attraction is mutual. Y receives X's letter on diagonally torn foolscap, short lines increasing to normal toward the bottom: X in the graphic mess of her kitchen gliding over a polenta in tomato sauce toward matters of women + the avant-garde. Y's fervid map, thus soon to be threading a path South from Montréal QC to Berkeley CA. The stucco house, complete with ace-of-spades-shaped entrance. And odd-shaped

35

silver-tinged Pacific plants around the garden. In back, a garage where X is working as publicist for the improvisational Rova Saxophone Quartet. Y sniffs avant-garde *everywhere! At X's party, she confabs with New Narrative writers Kevin Killian + Dodie Bellamy, Dodie quipping that she, prose writer, had to cross a barricade to attend this Language Poet party. New Narrative movement co-founder Robert Glück is absent—busy, someone says, establishing a new couple. This seems cool to everyone save Y. She wants OUT of hers, feels that a revolutionary must deploy all sorts of shifts + dodges, eccentric life styles, to function under the radar of the conventional. She brushes aside whether a queer household may be considered 'usual.' Days, Y strolls dreamily to background cafés in malls + parks. Everywhere in Berkeley, TV news reveling in O. J. Simpson's trial for murder of his Caucasian wife. People arguing noisily for one side or the other.*

It was thrilling for me to find writers in English working in parallel fashion to my French-language Montréal cohorts. The full-throated unabashedly cunty anger of Dodie Bellamy. And Camille Roy's nerdy street-smart lesbian = exemplary Fe-male versions of rage/resistance. As one who has also loved too much, I found Bob Glück's artily devastating love collages, their formal hybridity + underlying metafiction preoccupations, perfectly akin to my own prose efforts. Bob was to write: *The New Narrative writers were fellow travelers of Language Poetry and the innovative feminist poetry of that time, but our lives and reading led us toward a hybrid aesthetic, something impure.*[3] Oddly, however, I had already written my most novel-like novel. I was moving away from narrative in the usual sense. Felt in some ways, going forward, more a sister or daughter of pre–New Narrative author Kathy Acker's written violent disjunct body splatted all over the page—combining, sometimes hilariously, theory/discourse with sex. At a San Francisco performance of Carla Harryman's dramaturgy for *A Little Girl Dreams of Taking the Veil*[4], my first Acker encounter had the psychological hoops of a Chekhov story:

Y approaches the theatre. Full of anticipation: the performance has everything: text by surrealist Max Ernst, music by a local composer of experimental music, X's dramaturgy. Acker, resplendent in shaved blond head, piercings, etc., is outside, yelling for some reason, at X's husband. Y enters + takes a seat in the front row. Acker takes the empty seat to her left. Shortly suggesting switching places with Y, who, unable to think of a reason to refuse, acquiesces. Now Y finds herself next to a woman literally spewing a terrible cold or flu. Back in Montréal...ill for weeks.

My other Mothers, whom someone dubbed the masturbating French dykes—Wittig, Cixous, Irigaray—offered heady, brilliantly executed formulas for the excess in which my Montréal writing group bathed. There was also—significantly, for this essay—Colette Peignot, aka *Laure*, George Bataille's girlfriend. While the New Narrative men + women in Bob Glück's workshop in San Francisco took Bataille as major influence, Gail, Nicole, France, Louky + the two Louises had been tracking—sans any knowledge of the San Francisco group—parallel concerns. Bob wrote: *Bataille was central to our project. He finds a counter-economy of rupture and excess that includes art, sex, war, religious sacrifice, sports events, ruptured subjectivity, the dissolution of bodily integuments—"expenditure" of all kinds. Bataille showed us how a bathhouse and a church could fulfill the same function in their respective communities.*[5] In the Montréal workshop, my impression was that Colette Peignot's *Les écrits de Laure* held significance equal to or greater than Bataille as far as providing a means of giving us access to our own experience.

Raised in the strictest of Catholic bourgeois families, Laure/
Colette's family priest—mirrored in Bataille's *L'Abbé C*—was a
frequent presence in her childhood home, his hand a frequent
presence under the little girl's skirt. Rebellious from the start,
she became a Commie, lived in Russia a time, + with boyfriend
Georges, explored eroticism's limits, especially the complex
mix of Eros + Thanatos he championed. In her transgressive
text "The Sacred," Laure conflated eros + the sacred as a gesture
of resistance to capitalism's *commodification* of one's relation to
both the spiritual + the physical. *The sacred is for me that extremely
rare moment when the portion of the eternal we each carry within us,
enters life, sweeps us into the movement of the universe, integrale, fulfilled...* 6 It amused me to think, growing up part of my youth in
a half-French town, that Catholics had no problem in conjoin-
ing excess in spiritualism + eroticism. A Francophone feminist
poet friend [pert short hair, perfect straight back, flat tummy,
tall determined walk, even pushing 80], looks puzzled when I
suggest Laure was victimized in her situation with Bataille. She
prefers to speak of Laure's lack of a positive rapport with her
writing milieu. Laure knew she lacked scale. From my pinnacle
of having recently come out, Laure seemed isolated. George
had his cronies. Despite her attempts to experience a notion
of liberty in step with her male peers, she was not an interlocutor on an equal playing field with the men she frequented. Nor
did she appear to be a familiar of, say, the irrepressible Natalie
Barney crowd. I saw her as an alienated heterosexual woman
who died young. One could also say she strove to be *incontournable* but remained in the gaze of her cohorts, inherently a skirt,
notwithstanding continual anguish + struggle.

Still, right up to her death from TB in her mid-30s, her declared modus operandi was not to suppress joy but to exalt it; insolence + discomfort leaked out at every turn. She railed against 'goodness' + 'niceness.' My favourite quote: *The greatest potential in pulling off a crime/is knowing you can deny it/can fool everyone.*[7] Still, despite her efforts [+ this old story is familiar to so many females of the species]: Laure did not feel fulfilled. She wrote lines like *Georges, the most* Christian *I have been in my life...is when I have been with you.*[8] And on George's inevitable non-monogamy, which she of course accepted + emulated with energy + conviction, still she noted: ... *my nonchalance in speaking of your holidays as if the 6 weeks had flown by. My manner of altering posture, voice, tone. WRITE your books, make a novel of this poor being who only existed thanks to my JALOUSIE.*[9]

On that long-ago first trip to San Francisco, at a second-hand bookstore, Language Poet Barrett Watten thrust into my hands a beautiful early translation of formalist Viktor Shklovsky's *Zoo*. Like Beckett, but in more direct reference to the social, Shklovsky's Russian formalist devices of estrangement offered a means of tearing the picture from the false 'natural' or 'normal' of its context. Of setting it in relief with respect to a context constructed by dominant interests. In the multiple shadows of unexpressed possibilities in my own ongoing conversation with extremely variable continental contexts of reception, *Zoo* was instructive. It offered a way to follow the New Narrative example of threading the deeply personal through with borrowed materials from high + low culture—albeit more disjunct than many of the San Francisco crew. Vis-à-vis the Americans, I could not, among other things, distill the American genius for popular culture tropes into my work. As did Bob. Nor did I wish to. Russia was a Northern country, like Québec, + something about the late 20th left-leaning geopolitics—or perhaps just the extremes of climate—fit. It is in cumulative microcosmic ways that the facets of our solidarities are altered according to the place from which we speak. To be angry to the point of extreme—+ yet full of joy—as was Laure's generation, + ours, is to strike out beyond a pre-emptive + stifling *real*—in response to + shaped by imperatives of different milieux of reception. One needed to write in a way that offered a plurality of readings. [A telling example: Carla Harryman's hearing a screech in the little Francophone girl's *Eeeeeeeeengleeesh* at the end of *The Obituary*. Whereas I, in writing, intended to convey a soft French accent.]

My cohort France Théoret best explained the stakes of my hometown writing milieu in a novel called *Nous parlerons comme on écrit* [*One Day We Will Speak As We Write*], a title bearing as subtext North American French's phenomenal struggle to survive on an indifferent Anglo continent [meanwhile suffering the disdain of the Euro-French for the French spoken here]. Language was everywhere, a daily life-size foregrounding matter of conflict + pride in the general population. Even today, I am not the only one walking down the street practising the different accents I hear, the better to don one suitable to the moment, the neighbourhood.

Our particular way of speaking le féminin—contiguous with the struggle for a thriving French language in Québec—was part of what oriented our writing along other vectors than the San Francisco group. We, for instance, spoke of l'écriture + would, I think, have held to Barthes's early comment: *It is because there is no thought without language, that Form is the first and last arbiter of literary responsibility, and it is because there is no reconciliation within the present society, that language, necessary and necessarily orientated, creates for the writer a situation fraught with conflict.*[10] Authorship involved less narrator than writing subject for us; the difference was a question of degree, a matter of how composition became embedded in culture's multiple digressive referents.

To be writing in this context 'as a woman' soon produced yet another complicating matter in our Montréal conversations: Wittig's declaration: *Lesbians are not women*[11] fed my discomfort with Cixous's term *l'écriture féminine*, which carried, it seemed to me, the risk of projecting preconceived notions of what *to be a woman* can mean. Louky Bersianik, I think, came up with the term *l'écriture-AU-féminin*, which seemed refreshingly procedural in exploring whatever small or large portion of le féminin is relevant in a particular writer's trajectory. In French, I remember her saying, *le* féminin is a noun in the masculine gender—i.e., gender purity is impossible. Which, of course, the queers knew very well. But I don't think we have talked enough about the feminist/queer cusp.

Anecdote: Visiting San Francisco, I go with my then-girlfriend Dianne to an LGBTQ film festival at the Castro. As I recall, we saw a double bill: *Ticket of No Return* by Ulrike Ottinger and *Jeanne Dielman, 23, quai du Commerce, 1080 Bruxelles* by the late great Chantal Akerman. I think Bob happened to be sitting nearby. I don't remember the conversation we had about the two movies. I do remember Dianne + I were blown away by the Ottinger film: a woman buys a one-way ticket, flies to Berlin with a suitcase full of wild designer clothes, very imposing brightly coloured, odd-shaped gowns + hats, + proceeds day by day to drink herself to death. The clothes looked fantastic against the backdrop of grim subway walls and rathole Berlin bars, but what is really amazing is her ongoing performance, singing as if in a Brecht play, unsteadily dancing, dialoguing day after day until, in increasingly poor garments, still oh so tastefully put together, she dies, plummeting in flimsy white down a subway staircase. Set against Ottinger's formally unbridled excess was Akerman's perfect art object: a single mother, a rather dowdy prostitute, repeating the same gestures of domesticity + paid afternoon fucking + dinner + daily constitutional walk with son. Round + round they go, a perfectly heart-rending construction, until she suddenly murders a client who's taking too long to come. This was art as we most admire it: a certain rigour I love + perhaps envy. But it was Ottinger's work that made me think of Jane Bowles's zany tales, of Sheila Watson's clipped irony. Of Louky Bersianik's brilliant, wildly effervescent women from outer space, or picnicking on the Acropolis in place of the *male* philosophers.

To marry the Ottinger brand of excess with the defamiliarizing compositional qualities of a Shklovsky seemed a means to shift from individual self-expression toward a mode where the text is no longer the psychological arc that is a feature of the novel form. Gleaning from everywhere, Shklovsky's *Zoo* is an epistolary novel moving in a series of overlapping frames; author *affect* is distanced by a deployment of formal devices: reversals, disjunctions, cross-outs, humour, etc. There may not be narrative in this work, or narrative may be embedded in there somewhere, but it is not the be-all + end-all. It may be supplied by the reader. The writer John

Keene once asked me a brilliant question: how did the *Theory, A Sunday* group rinse the sentimentalism out of queer? I suppose the answer might have been that we combined fiction AND theory. It certainly did not damage our trajectory that for a time, in order to free ourselves of certain preconceived canonical notions, some of us read mostly women, including the great women philosophers of the era. *Women. And poets*, interjected Nicole Brossard.

I will finish with a citation that sent me on the path toward experimental prose in my salad years, prior to meeting the New Narrative group, or even the *Theory, A Sunday* group: Québécois Hubert Aquin's *Next Episode*, written while confined in a psychiatric hospital [instead of prison, for radical political action], where he dreamed of post-revolutionary Cuba.

Cuba is sinking into flames in the middle of Lac Léman while I descend to the bottom of things. Packed inside my sentences, I glide, a ghost, into the river's neurotic waters, discovering as I drift the underside of surfaces and the inverted image of the Alps. Between the anniversary of the Cuban Revolution and the date of my trial, I have time enough to ramble on in peace....[12]

CORPUS DELICTI

Translators are none other than the High Ransomers of foreign
cultures. In the process of holding one culture ransom, they (I could
just as easily say we) find themselves brandishing ransom notes for
at least as many of the cultures as are attributed to the languages in
which they work, exposing in the process, the foreignness *of every*
culture, and their distance from what they might be inclined to call
their own.
—Nathanaël, translator/poet[1]

…if the notion of universal thinking…has been so magnificently
and fulsomely realized in Western history, is this way of thinking
still in itself, as a system, equal to offering fresh perspectives for the
world in which we now live?
—Édouard Glissant[2]

The buried speech that creates a soundless gap between languages is at the heart of life in multilingual cities [which is most of them]. And of translation. The translator is an ally, ideally working languages in extension of each other. Making, through decontextualizing, meaning. To make France Théoret's *Laurence* sound in English as it does in French—with its breathless run-on French phrasing—many sentences were turned around completely. So there is a reverse Alice-in-the-looking-glass kind of 'Reality' to the relationship between the two. Reversal helped, as well, to keep the scenes appearing small, at a distance, for the novel is a series of miniature tableaux. Before the sentences could be turned, they had to be *heard*. To have collaborated on various projects with Théoret for more than a decade, particularly on questions of language + gender in a context of cultural proximity, enhanced my sense of cultural particularities + cadences. And facilitated translation of the so-called 'natural' that still haunts the novel form. I think of this as putting body sounds into syntax. *However*, as looking-glass Alice liked to say:

HOWEVER:

The Reality of language A, with its rules + regulations, its cadences, its strategies for creating a simulacrum, may be, by that very fact or act, unacknowledging of the Reality of neighbouring language B, its practices and everyday realities. If we are, on this continent, speaking of translation or translinguistic phenomena in a 'universally' Anglo-dominant context, then for the minority speaker or cultural group, the transference into the realm of the purported universal can be fraught with loss. As James Baldwin said: *For a black writer, especially in this country* [the U.S.], *to be born into the*

English language is to realize that the assumptions on which the language operates are his enemy.[3] He goes on, in a 1979 Berkeley lecture, to draw a link between language + the Civil Rights uprisings of that 60s/70s era. *If you need to fight for Civil Rights you are not a Citizen.* To speak a certain way is proof of belonging.

Pre-coded as sound [speech, song, movement], what the translator is summoned to reproduce in her language is what she grasps from the *other* body of evidence. But how to write the living 'ear' of a phrase, to create within the parameters of the dominant language's illusions + presumptions, the body/Memory of the original's sum of conditions, its oozing speech inflections + word relations, its particular fashioning of sentences? And fashioning's impact on meaning. Can she the translator write more than she hears? More than she has lived in the Habitus that is her own culture? And does it matter? The drift of meaning from one site to another can produce, notably where some sort of proximity is actual, where one language is not suppressed by the other, texts of incredible + complex beauty.

To be opening out toward the horizons of the global perhaps requires more reflection on translinguistic gaps, on the impact of language moving from one context to another. A bad [impatient] translation [or translinguistic misapprehension] appropriates what it can of the Other according to its own structure of meanings, values. In which case, one might ask: Is translation a heist? Is it a love affair where the top [to borrow a queer erotic term] is overweening, possessive? Is it, less dramatically, a love affair where one panders + the other maintains intractable reserve? Is it indifference, betrayal? Is it a beautiful solidarity among equals?

What does it mean that translation on this planet moves majoritarily toward English? Which is the primary language of capitalist exchange. And Indigenous genocide. On this real-time continent, at least from the Rio Grande to the reaches of the Arctic, English—the legacy of conquest—has won. And still mostly does. What gets left behind?

EXHIBIT A: THE UNIVERSAL + ITS LABYRINTHS: Let us trace a pyramid of imperialism, topped by Europe, where suppressed languages—la langue d'Oc, for instance—have long been laundered in the universalizing syntaxes of nation-states. Where, at any rate, contemporary perceptual differences between French, say, + German are modest, compared to the gap between European + non-European languages. Yet, to look at the distinct place of the verb, in respective French or German sentencing, is to note that thought may in these proximities trace 2 substantively different patterns.

To wit: French translator Jean Daive's struggles in his memoir, *Sous la coupole*.[4] The work, covering two decades of friendship + translation with German-language poet Paul Celan, reads as a besotted lover's tale of endlessly short-circuited intimacy—operating at precisely the point where translation meets the personal meets poetry: that is, at the edge of the incommunicable. The memoir's tale of frustrated desire to penetrate the spoken + textual of two major European languages features two cisgender European males, each fluent in the other's mother tongue. Who, walking + talking under the leafy dome of Paris streets + parks, become a trope for translation's often awkward performative reaches, flounderings. As if to imply that to translate is to necessarily function under the sign of *maladresse*, Daive writes: *The shop windows seem to reflect sad dreams. He walks and makes elusive phantom signs. Conversation is impossible. On the other hand, we make no noise.*[5] Perhaps embittered, he remarks that Celan's French is stilted, i.e., German-inflected. [And this may be further complicated by the fact that Celan spoke German at home, but grew up in Romania, a Jew who understood Yiddish + was taught Hebrew.] Celan, Daive complains, is like the tethered donkey that he watches two decades later, while in the process of penning his memoir on a Greek Island: Celan, complains the French translator, augments distance by remaining "a static image." Though he [the donkey!] *cries, he weeps, he brays*, what the chronicler Daive hears, in the untranslatable braying, is the loss of what he desires—as *the still living mass fall(s) into the sea, into the Seine* [Celan's suicide]. Written in prose fragments that often recall, in tone, the self-involved discursive language acts of *Nouvelle Vague* cinema—the memoir suggests another issue troped by the melancholy of the besmitten: the tendency of translation to be immanently self-conscious. In the later American-English translation of *Under the Dome*, German-American translator Rosmarie Waldrop excavates Daive's self-consciousness by choosing to emphasize, precisely, the sentimental awkwardness of his performance as enamoured second. Waldrop, fluent in all 3 languages, underscores this with the phrase

—*There is a trap. There is a trap between Paul and me.*[6]

The English "There is a trap between Paul and me" is odd. Speculating on the French version, which I have not seen, I might have said: "There is an abyss..." But Waldrop, also a poet, does not water the surface language for the sake of message; she takes it to the other extreme, + in so doing, reveals the text's most profound measure.

THERE IS A TRAP.

Unable to keep Celan from augmenting distance by disappearing into the obliquity of his own interior, Daive, in his inimitable French way of seeing things for what they are even as he suffers, strives to maintain an ironic distance. *I listen. I listen above all to his jerky diction that detaches every word, almost every syllable. The words so detached plunge into a state of waiting that indefinitely prolongs my listening. Paul creates an aquarium effect that muffles what he communicates, makes it hard to hold on to, hold on to immediately.*[7]

//

EXHIBIT B: THE MIDDLE GROUND: In my town, Montréal, QC, it can feel like the French language is the survivor of 2 colonial impulses, Euro-French + continental English. Walking the streets, trying different French accents to find what suits best in any local social stratum, I find that the farther east I go, the more a Québécois tonality seems applicable. Whereas I who live in the centre of the city where the cultures meet, speak a middle ground of fairly international + slightly Anglo-accented French. So why do I, an Anglo, when in Paris, pelt the ears of the Euro-French with every Québécois expression I can muster? Quaint to some [a young Parisian poet reporting laughing all the way home on the métro]; to others, rustic, provincial: Why am I performing self-deMEaning for language-snob Parisians? Is it the only way to appear 'authentic' in my second language? My Franco-Québécois friends, writers, teachers, etc., speak international French, at home + abroad. An American in Paris one day declaring I mispronouncing rue de Lille—my short Québécois ï sounding rue de *lïl*. It's rue de *leel*, she exclaims. I laugh at an *American* correcting, with her *American* accent, my *Québécois* French…. In a Paris translation workshop reading, I recite a Québécois drinking song in alternate Québécois + English. Calling out the lines, full of Montréal argot, in the rhythm of a jig. People are laughing, *with me*, I think…. Then worry it may be *at*. I leave early….

//

EXHIBIT C: CIRCUMSTANTIAL EVIDENCE: *THIS* translator/lover of her translingual Montréal context is *no whining Anglo* wanting accommodations. What she wants is her *city to be French*—notwithstanding certain indications to the contrary. For one, a tone-deaf Anglo-Montréal propensity to cast the city as bilingual. Complicated by the arrival of so many new accents from everywhere on the planet. So when an American friend comes to visit, this translator/lover sets out to prove her city French. Said visitor perhaps already dubious, having arrived, French dictionary in hand, left over from a junior year abroad, to find his halting French receiving—from a too-hospitable customs agent—a reply in perfect English.

Like Jean + Paul, Montréal Gail + San Francisco Bob walk. From the former working-class east, the first electoral districts to support the nascent 1970s Québec independence option. West toward the cosseted mansions of traditionally Anglo-dominant Westmount. True, both parts of town are increasingly multicultural. But it's apéritif hour, so instead of heading west to the historic higher Anglo reaches, we cut north, across Mount Royal's grassy eastern foot, to a chi-chi bar frequented by a well-heeled, Outremont, mostly Francophone clientele [some of whose grandparents shamelessly hobnobbed with the English, the better to make their fortunes, while subsequent generations plotted just as shamelessly to overturn them—even to the point of committing acts of terrorism]. The late afternoon is filled with a *joie de vivre* Anglos are wont to call *Latin*. Dutifully refreshed, Gail suggests a tour to the Haitian/Latinx north, to prove her city can be multicultural in French. But the guest's patience may be wearing thin with all these explanations. Unabashed, she leads him to the multi-ethnic Main [boul. St-Laurent], meeting place of the city's binaries, anomalies. Unfortunately, when Gail orders two Boréale Blondes in French, the waiter, whose mother tongue is Portuguese, uncooperatively replies in English, perhaps to show that his second-language English is less accented than her second-language French. Curiously, younger Québécois Francophones, children + grandchildren of those radical Québécois indépendantistes, are likewise inclined to respond—to even the slightest Anglo accent or appearance—in English. This is unfortunate for one who wants to write with French in her ear to frame her own language/culture from a certain critical distance. *This posture of perpetual doubt,* she tells her American friend, *some may call postmodern. I call it the cacophony of realism. —I get it,* he replies. *You live in exile. Like Stein. Hemingway.* This makes her angry. Is not she, in her writing, an exemplary Citizen of this place?

Who reads your work? asks the American, ever practical, twisting the ends of his moustache between his fingers. Having finishcd a plate of excellent lamb couscous in an Algerian eatery, they are walking toward the *pont Jacques-Cartier*, punctuating the horizon in the beginning of its long arc or comma over the river.

Tomorrow, Gail will expand on the comma of translation—that space that signals the perpetual human drift of identity. Which he understands well, being himself 'a bit of a queen.' In the gay village, he disappears into a showbar for men only. She sits in a café watching tourists, leather dykes. Throngs of beautiful men in tight sweaters + good haircuts. The queens decked out as Nana Mouskouri, or the eternal Marilyn. The trans-women, coiffed, well turned-out, attractively skirted, climbing stairs to a bar suitably named Sky. Tomorrow she + he will talk of what it means to write with unstable identities. He is interested in writing where women becoming men. Men becoming women. Men becoming men. Women becoming women. Of what it means, each in our own trajectories. He will add some brilliantly offhand "2 cents worth." Such as... *Queer voice is a conceptual puddle.* And she will note that, as Glissant says of the poet, one may be working with general language parameters, one does not necessarily obey them. Which is why she will continue to let Québécois French interrupt, subvert her work, continue to challenge that dominatrix, English. English can handle it. *Oui, Madame!!*

//

EXHIBIT D: INDIFFERENCE. BETRAYAL [+ HERE'S THE RUB!]: Fact: Many of the continent's cities have Indigenous names. Names like little flags sticking up in the midst of climate-heating high-rise concrete, trying to cover loss/plunder by those operating on behalf of Big Capital. However, no assertive nor stated criminal intent does not mean no crime. To be craving a chunk of the other—their knowledge, their land, their artifacts, thereby triggering centuries of cruelly decreed death or assimilation—is to force one group into a situation of perpetual translation from sites of radically different values, alphabets. If the violent cross-over impact is starting to be acknowledged, there is alas no real inclination to provide the economic possibilities [return of land + resources] to start remedying the calamity.

In this abyss between the very ancient + the recent colonizing cultures is also found the many whose origins have been in part obfuscated by the assimilate-or-die legacy of settler culture. And who can no longer assert a belonging on paper, or culturally, in the sense of tribal connections. If heritage is knowledge, such lacking of knowledge/experience of an ancestral culture may indicate claims of little relevance. Certainly some, being lost, try to make exaggerated claims; others feel profound embarrassment vis-à-vis those claiming some degree of Indigeneity on the basis of a distant ancestor:

No matter what I say I feel a liar. After my maternal grandmother died Grandpa told my brother our Grandma was Métis. Other relatives deny it. During her lifetime nary a word. I have a single memory of a neighbour calling her a squaw. Grandpa, while not in the closet about his mixed background, foregrounded his being American (from Kansas). We were left with threads: he was born to a family of horse people. They moved north + raised horses for the Crowsnest Pass coal mines. But the history of their origins has disappeared in the dust. How many grow up like this? Does it matter? One could also ask: When does a language cease to be written on the body?[8]

It is worth recalling that the impact of cultural cannibalization works in two directions. A number of no-longer-spoken or little-spoken suppressed Indigenous tongues infuse/alter or add another layer of matter to plundering English. And those who would have spoken these violently suppressed languages, or who do, yet have little option but to write in the language of the colonizer, bringing via their persons, their values, their heartbeats, lines, sentences, cadences, compositions that are other. I am wont to praise the beauty of such texts. But is not that, in itself, a colonial comportment? Wanting to be a good fellow traveller, the translator tries to calm her doubt by pointing out that there is a fundamental difference between writing by Indigenous authors in English who are rooted in their culture. And that of individuals with fuzzy or murky claims to Indigeneity. A difference that shows up, among others, in language cadence. Recently, for instance, I have been blown away by the genial dialoguing in Haisla + Heiltsuk writer Eden Robinson's *Son of a Trickster,* a masterful representation of speech in the realm of text.

For me writing is a matter of ear: it is what one hears in words on a page that takes work out of the straitjacket of commodifying literary conventions. Words work differently on the page—sometimes a little differently, sometimes a lot—when translated from oral culture, or from writing in one language with other languages impacting it [a lesson I have learned writing in Montréal]—even in cases where these languages are no longer widely spoken. Attention to words sitting differently in the English language is what I hear in the work of so many First Nations writers. Louise Bernice Halfe, to mention only one, because she is a trailblazer, + uses Cree in her English-language work to great effect, + is a woman + one of the most amazing poets. Also, it is from her that I heard the expression of words sitting differently in language. It has happened that writers with weak claims of Indigenous belonging, be they authors of accomplished novels, but who lack a deep BODILY sense of language/culture, become laureates of the critical literary establishment. Indeed tokenism vis-à-vis minorities has often resulted in privileging that which most resembles the Canadian mainstream. *History belongs to the victors,* Walter Benjamin was fond of saying. It took the current waves of resistance headed by the *Idle No More* movement + a simultaneous cohort of dazzling Indigenous writers to see more clearly that values are communicated in scaffolding of a novel; in how one moves through space + notions of time. In the relations between sentences + in the meaning of 'individual' or person. Writers rooted in non-European language backgrounds, sound different in English. And this is beautiful. The best critics—and the best translators—have ears.

Speaking of ears, good intentions can run afoul: Our translator, in her novel, *The Obituary*, which is precisely about buried roots + assimilation, shamefully misspells the book's sole Indigenous word,: *Oligawi* (sleep well), as *Ogigawa,* mistaking in translating the oral [from a conversation with an Abenaki woman] to the written. For one, hearing 'l' as ' g'. It is the critic, Stan Dragland, in a kind text about our translator's 'difficult' writing, who points out *Ogigawa* is in fact a Japanese word. Two things interest our translator about this:

1. How, in moving from one language to another, the ear, locked in its own cadences, mishears. An English speaker, for instance, tends to pronounce written 't's at the end of certain French words, so that *lentement* (slow, in French, pronounced lāt.mā) is erroneously pronounced *lant-mant.*

2. How, in looking online, under the thick layer of dominant Western languages with their residual strength of imperialism, it seemed at first impossible to find an Abenaki word for *goodbye* that resembled in the least the word she thought she'd heard. She even cross-referenced her search with geographically proximate Indigenous languages—falling at last, quite by accident, upon the Abenaki word for *dream well (Oligawi)*. So the woman with whom she had been in conversation on the way home from the grocer was saying not *goodbye* as she presumed. But perhaps a form of *good night?*

Thus one settler-culture ignorance piles upon another, ignorance in which the translator is often, willy-nilly complicit: *We rest our case.*

THE SUTURED SUBJECT

habitual placement of the tongue changes the mouth//
when the tongue is still, are you quiet enough to hear the
dead? quiet enough to hear the land stifled beneath massive
concrete? quiet enough to hear the beautiful, poisoned
ancestors surfacing from your diaphragm?
the reigning voice resigns or resignifies
—Rita Wong[1]

//

I can never write the novel I want. In the absence of visible constellations on my night street, only dim rays leak from cracks + keyholes in the heavenly crypt above. The overwhelming brightness of the city, one of most lit on the continent, has devoured the starry night.

Not novel then—let's just say...*ventriloquism?* The puppet sitting on magician's knee glittering with narrative possibilities. But who really speaks when she, the puppet, speaks? Can she channel the dead? In the epigraph to my novel *The Obituary*, post-Freudian psychoanalysts Abraham + Torok suggest, rather, that...*what haunts are not the dead but the gaps left within us by the secrets of others....* Thereby shifting emphasis from the interiority of the individual as per Freud's bourgeois [+ our contemporaneous *middle-class*] family onto the scene of the social. Their investigation of language as a site where endogenous meets exogenous ran parallel to 20th-century avant literary excavations of the act of writing, aimed at moving away from an individualist notion of subject, fostered [as I see it] in domestic childhood education. While, from Dada/Surrealism to later Language Poetry, queer New Narrative, + what Québec women have called fiction/theory, writing experimentation has been consumed with the task of retooling the writing subject, embedding her in the social + in the collective effort we call language. In other words, prying her away from the incipient individualism of middle class aspirations. It is worth noting these movements have generally appeared in moments of radical social transition—or dreams thereof. Where there is no emergency, there is likely no real experiment.

METHOD: Rilke's experiments involving reading coronal suture are reported by Kittler: *A trace or a groove appears where the frontal + parietal bones of the suckling infant have grown together,* wrote Rilke. As if, commented Kittler, the facilitations of Freud + Exner had been projected out of the brain onto its enclosure,[2] the naked eye is now able to read the coronal suture as a writing of the real. Apply a gramophone needle to said coronal sutures, or *to any anatomical surface*, + what they yield, upon replay, is a primal sound without a name, music without notation, a sound ever more strange than any incantation for the dead for which the skull might have been used. Instead of making fervent melancholic associations with the skeleton, the markings traced on the cylinder are, for the writer, physiological traces. Implying that our own nervous system, our own body = the outside world. To attempt to read + write this notion of suture or splice is to attempt to juxtapose memory/body/gesture onto languages of the street, of media, of reading.

If the word *spliced* has here supplemented the word *sutured* the debt is to Fred Moten's Glenn Gould essay "Sonata Quasi Una Fantasia." Moten's discussion of splicing treats the act of closing a gap in a manner concomitant with digital media practices, + music. Moten notes that the splice follows a suspension of narrative, a caesura that breaks down the anticipated arc of meaning, multiplying possibilities, thus narrative vectors. *To be truthful to yourself is a contrapuntal task that manifests itself as multiple solitude in fictional splice.*[3]

In my novel, *The Obituary*, investigation of suppressed Indigeneity on a specific site *attempts* to suture torn edges of both urban + ancestral remembrance. In the process, producing a speaker who's less persona or character than 3-pronged fractal. Whether laying expired or passed out on the bed, or embodying a fly dancing on the wall, or preaching from the basement, the torn edges of the Rosine figure open space for a polyphonic ventriloquy. Emitting—one could say—as if from the psychoanalytic couch + its telling perambulations, located half on the street. The grainy death-dream street in Ingmar Bergman's *Wild Strawberries*, its gauzy black-+-white dream eruption into the narrative of the technicolour 60s film, sent me dancing home, age 17, from some repertory cinema. The segment's almost corny stopped clock, free-rolling wagon wheel, etc., gave licence in the way it sliced a hole in the procedure to step outside prevailing narratives as regards *both* everyday life + my soon fledgling project of art exploration. I was a little shaken by the film segment's contrived strangeness. Death as in the Tarot, auguring endings but, *also*, new beginnings. I have always loved the Grim Reaper's grin. Writing *The Obituary*, it seemed essential to mix dead + living in tight syntactic + narrative proximity. Allowing—in contrast to the Western life/death binary—city + family ghosts who had lost ties to their history, moving about in urban space, fully fleshed. My 'sutured subject' thus a fictional splice, to borrow Moten's term again—although in practice no doubt falling short of Moten's profound musicality—of sound, texture, + traces of collective memory. Mixed with those urban voices that attempted to capture my particular shame-filled Montréal site of unceded territory. This is our history, its inoperable arc decomposing into a detective-genre type quest to reconnoitre not roots but a way to knit together, as subjects with 'inchoate' origins, our criminally splayed edges. Alas... *Whole tale's omissions contributing to succeeding generations' inability to communicate with open-mindedness, understanding, steadfastness of principles, consequently, always putting up defence walls of near paranoia.*[4] The tale, being set in Francophone Québec, but starring an Eeeengleesh [as the protagonist Rosine is tagged by a little Francophone girl at a party], makes the entire procedure—+ its 'teller'—suspect. A photo of a small mixed-race girl, supposedly the mother of Rosine as a child, is the most direct reference to the tale's 'omissions.'

SATURATION: What the trope of stopped clock represents—caesura, disjunction, estrangement—seems during this terrible 2020 pandemic summer, this watershed era of Black + Indigenous uprisings—saturated from repeated use. Or, more likely—I submit—from too cautious application. As with social struggle, failure to break the formal chain of authority, of its aesthetic as well as its social relations, its ritualized meanings, can dampen a hope that begins with inspired youthful explosions. The culture worker is always at risk of slipping into the neo-liberal mainstream. When, for example, an innovative scriptor gains cultural capital, the pressure of kudos such as literary prizes function as arbiters of genre, glazing a work in prestige discourse. Often glazing in turn the artist, as she morphs, little by little, into a posture of doing as is expected, the better to maintain her status. Mina Loy, mocking in her art + in her political struggles, half-measures such as the idea that women should be content with rising in the professions, asked: *Is that all you want?* Her advice to feminists: *There is no half-measure—NO scratching on the surface of the rubbish heap of tradition, will bring about **Reform**, the only method is **Absolute Demolition**. Cease to place your confidence in economic legislation, vice-crusades & uniform education—you are glossing over **Reality**.*[5]

But is not there always some kind of dance between reform + revolution? Bob Glück, co-editor with myself, Camille Roy, + Mary Berger of the New Narrative anthology *Biting the Error*, had, for instance, early on called *the poetry of disjunction…a luxurious idealism in which the speaking subject rejects the confines of representation and disappears in the largest freedom, that of language itself.*[6] His workshop of queer men + women, having been disastrously represented in the mid-to-late 20th-century mainstream, therefore insisted that... *Political agency required at least a provisionally stable identity!* Precisely what WE the *Theory, A Sunday* group were saying at the same time. Freedom for US required another recipe.

US... The empathy button lights in my ancient militant's head. And there's my hungry treacherous self, again, ever wandering in search of stimulus + conversation. I.e., literary comrades. Leaving Montréal, where the second 1995 independence referendum defeat had flattened an already fading general revolutionary impulse. First to Paris [a failed search for a lost avant-garde—but some good conversations with the ghosts of Gertrude Stein + Walter Benjamin]. Then to late-90s San Francisco. On to post-millennial New York. Having already ca 1980 left Anglo- for Franco-Québec, to go to NY was to follow in the traces of several other Montréal creators over time [artist Moyra Davey, cartoonist Julie Doucette, Leonard Cohen]. Manhattan's hyper-energized air of the Obama years indeed provided conversations about the relationship of art to radical politics that I yearned for. Isn't it *always* a matter of conversation? The more intense, the better. New Conceptualist poet [+ psychoanalyst] Kim Rosenfield's perspicacious *Bomb* interview questions, for instance:

> KR: *What struck me when I began reading* The Obituary *was the epigraph you used by Abraham & Torok: what haunts are not the dead but the gaps left within us by the secrets of others. Their ideas of the Phantom, of the crypt, seem like the ideal theoretical frame for exploring your novel. In fact I'd like to use their thinking to guide this interview....*

GS: ... *Lisa Robertson introduced me to Abraham and Torok, during a visit to Vancouver. I was telling her about the quandary of writing a work to do with shame in assimilated families, yet adamantly not wanting to do an identitary or quest novel. My prose has been concerned with the redistribution of narration over a broken or accidented topography in order to trouble conventional relations of narrator, narration, narrative. I have been avoiding using, as best I can, unary voiced narration by sharding character to allow a maximum porosity or absorption of noise and text along a line where intrinsic and extrinsic meet. To use elements of family history was to risk getting stuck in a conventional rendering of the past (nostalgia). The critical notion that I retained from reading* The Shell and the Kernel *was the notion of ventriloquism, which treats the speaking voice as a conduit of multiple voices, past and present, endogenous and exogenous. This allows the unconscious chorus of previous generations and their social conditions to be deployed as part of the present racket. If the chorus remains repressed in the family or historical narrative, then whatever or whoever steps on stage to speak, has all her unresolved anger and shame stowed away in a secreted gap within, like walking around with a foreigner in her stomach. How perfect for a tale of cultural genocide, which is in so many ways a founding meta-narrative of continental North American culture. What the novel turned out to be—something I always only learn at the end of writing—was an investigation of who speaks when one speaks.*[7]

Or—who has the right to speak? Who of the voices seeping up from one's past, from history, from the crypt that is family? That family, that cohort of prime consumers, so lauded by politicians across the generations. And by some feminists, the better to acknowledge, among other things, the huge unpaid role of women in the formation of the notion of Citizen. Certainly what happens in the Domus is germinal to one's becoming. The making of food, speech, manners, values, in the air of the Domus's particular erotics, the devoted mother-face in window, coded to foster, as per religious + nation-state ideology, the chestnut of happiness. And so it appears for many. But that alleged safe + warm + fuzzy space can also be debilitating, dangerous. *I am lying on my couch, wrapped in a pink fleece blanket, wondering what would happen if the austerity of the smash-the-state Revolution were a little more like the gentleness of coming home,* writes Tricia Low, in a stroke of ironic sensibility. Further suggesting that…*the end goal of revolution to feel cozy + familiar would likely end in some reformist compromise.*[8] Whether in front of our screens—contemporaneously an exogenizing factor of childhood education from a very early age—or whether having physically exited the Domus walls ['to exit' is always relative, represents a range of degrees]—socialization beyond the family threshold also weighs substantively for women. And, in a different way, for men, given that life's most productive energy is consumed by protecting, by eternally returning to uphold the little fortress. Certainly, queer children have traditionally suffered inordinately from Domus norms + role definitions. Fe-male that I am, I felt better—but also as if torn—in social collectives of resistance to standard comfort + commodiousness. One could also say:

WE ARE FAMILY. Sitting around the polished Outremont table of Nicole Brossard, whom we jokingly dub la mère Brossard [mère + maire/mayor sounding almost the same in French]—Nicole being more maire than mère. And there is France, same short New

Wave film haircut, same erect posture decades later; the queen of novels rigorously philosophical. And there is the ephemeral Louky's novel of a woman visiting our planet, horrified at how Earth treats its women. Also at the table, the two Louises, hailing from a site of class struggle called Thetford Mines. Moi, the Anglo, taller than the others, abruptly standing + banging into a pricey chandelier set lower than anticipated. Over the gleaming table scatter shattered modernist glass pieces, my cohorts' faces [save cool Nicole's] gazing up in horror. We had been discussing, perhaps, la *sujette* [roguely feminized term for *sujet*] —over café/croissants, later tongue-loosening wine/food. A little in the wake of Kristeva, each in our way seeking to be writing against integration into the *symbolic order*. Ferociously feminist [2 lesbians, 1 bi-, 3 straight], for a time some of us read mostly women authors, because it was necessary to address our kind if we were to write without censure. At the same time, we had in common with certain avant male poets the sense of writing from a semi-colonized space of partial, failed resistance to the suppression of Francophone culture.

Vancouver writer Meredith Quartermain + I recently discussed the presence of a north/south pole for Anglo Montréal + Vancouver artists.[9] In my case, going south, to be able to discuss in English my modest prose explorations was reassuring in two senses: English-language readers could grasp my work more readily than my Franco colleagues. As well, given the larger experimental prose network in the vast country called America, it offered more occasion to discuss with writers interested in issues of syntax/grammar. Prose writers who similarly experienced how vertical working of language in prose caused hesitation at the space between the period + the next sentence. Thanks to Gertrude Stein, there was also an interest in the effect on meaning of the French sentence's axis being the verb, whereas the English sentence seemed, at least to this Canadian, more oriented toward reaching its object.... *Each time I start, it's as if the memory of the past (the noun, the sentence's beginning) wipes out the present (verb). So I can no longer move forward in the words*, I wrote in *Heroine*. Could one name the crisis of fiction a result of the nervous breakdown of expectations in the department of relations between sentences? Renee Gladman was also saying experimental prose is about a crisis in semantics, not about psychological trauma, *though the latter is not excluded*.

SEMANTICS/AFFECT: One question for queer women, specifically: how to read/write a city? How to construct integral representation; to perform gestures of shifting in + out of shadows, streets? To self-present in a crowd of Others? Does one finger the fissures along the intrinsic/extrinsic terrain that is one person in relation to the common, until one's writing subject metonymizes into a kind of music, or floating gravity? But this seems too lyrical/romanticized.

—*Can't we just call it sex?* wrote Kathy Acker in signing a book for writer Dodie Bellamy, whose incredible sentence assemblages are cries of verve, anger, + droll negative allure. I love how that energy creates a perpetual *avant* performance motion. Dodie, like Eileen Myles, + other New Narrative prose writers, contributors to the Bellamy/Killian 2017 anthology, *Writers Who Love Too Much*,[10] sign an obsession with our own hysteria, our hesitation at the point of bifurcation situated somewhere between person + world. Might it be that the most radical impulse shared by experimental prose writers is a fixation on spaces among layers of narrative, + among sentences? Gladman [+ others] offer a temporal take on this process: to write sentences-in-becoming is to register the phenomenon of being-in-life, necessarily crossing genres, resulting, among other things, in the production of failed sentencing. Gladman insists on calling this failure—where a person can only be represented partially—not experimental fiction, but prose. Gladman asks, citing Bhanu Kapil Rider: *What happens when the person, jarred in repetition at the border, begins to speak?*[11] So much can be said about being jarred at the border. In the current political configuration, to be stuck at a border may mean your children ending up in a cage. Or, if any version of Fe-male, your head lodged against that glass ceiling. And if the border were grammatical?—what I precisely wanted to explore was the problem of proceeding from one utterance to the next. How to get the line to proceed beyond the enjambment but in a non-teleologic fashion? Gertrude Stein, whose immense art was also the art of a breezy upper-middle-class American, saw the sentence as her little dog lapping, only a lap, a measure, in the breath of a paragraph. So, no problem moving forward. I prefer to think of post–Russian Revolution formalist Viktor Shklovsky, who, after endless efforts to put together one of his novels, cut the pieces up + let them come together by chance. On the floor. And Beckett who over + over abandoned his long prose manuscripts, only to take them up again. Again. Again! Much of what gets determined about where the emphasis lies between language focus + other influences in the complex domain of contemporary narrative gets decided in those intervals, among or within sentences, where the vectors sink for a moment, into the unarticulable present. Instead of narrative, you get indeed something closer to assemblage. But for the Montréal feminists, + the San Francisco New Narrative writers, the writing subject is not an arty abstraction, might even be excessively fleshed in her clearly constructed or performed way. All this to say, how one organizes one's sentences, if they have any point at all, requires the aesthetic spilling into the social.

Experimental prose, wrote Language Poet Ron Silliman once upon a time, is among the most difficult work of all for people to gauge... Have recent decades' experiments in reading/writing + everyday life altered that situation? Or is this often difficult-seeming work offering resistance to both analog arcs + social media's rapid summations? How relevant vis-à-vis certain prescribed bromides is the diva of experimental narrative Kathy Acker's dissing of realism, by which she means a plotted narrative: ...*simply a control method. Realism doesn't want to negotiate, to open into....*[12] And she calls the chaos of the disjunct gappiness of her prose *interstices in our treasure hunt.* This, by the way, is resonant of the Artaud quote that inspired the title of the New Narrative anthology *Biting the Error*, which, as I write, is still, 15 years after publication, the leading experimental prose-essay anthology: *From this moment of* error—wrote Artaud—*there remains the feeling that I have snatched something real from the unknown.*[13] Here is a remarkably layered + torqued Acker version of the 'real' from her masterpiece *Empire of the Senseless*:

1) *When I regained consciousness, unlike the old cashew nut, I lifted up the first public phone receiver I could find...*

From the *Bomb* interview with Kim Rosenfield came another question re my novel *The Obituary*'s relation to the real.

KR: All of your novels use failure of containment (and maybe this is the gape, or the anomaly or shadow that you mention) as a stylistic choice. By that I mean your narrative(s) do not hold a usual sequence of events, do not hold time as continuous. This framing/un-framing speaks to your idea(s) of sutured subject...

*GS: ...if I were a poet, at least as far as the poetry I like to read, I would not feel the need to re-suture. I would not feel the need to create a docu-semblance of reality, while reconnoitering what Fred Wah brilliantly terms—and in his case accomplishes—*Music at the Heart of Thinking. *To try to operate at the limits of articulation, which is one of our tasks as writers, is to perform spillage with respect to whatever genre or field in which one is working. Gertrude Stein is so right when she says it is never beautiful the first time—*Of course it is beautiful but first all beauty in it is denied and then all the beauty of it is accepted. *I like that she puts the onus on the reader to find the beauty. With respect to the novel genre, the narration in* The Obituary *is embedded, perhaps even submerged along the way in something closer to composition, in order to foreground the possibilities of language in excess of the usual predominant communicative vectors of a tale. But I also feel a desire to at least pretend that I am sewing the bits together in a semblance of narrative, while leaving the accidented relations between the parts obvious. Poetry does this. Why cannot I and still call it a novel?*[14]

A delightful example of narrative linked to rescuing the vexed queer/feminist subject—indeed, shifting subject into what the New Conceptualists called *SOBJECT*—is this passage from Glück's story "The Purple Men." Concerning an alleged scientific experiment where the anuses of two men are painted with an invisible dye; + scientists watch them slowly turning purple as they come.

They are not entirely purple yet. They have purple shadows and the space around them protects and amplifies their nakedness with pinks and salmons of undifferentiated flesh. One man reaches through the other's crotch to pin down a wrist, getting a spot of purple, I guess, on his forearm. The scene may be naturalistic, but it conveys the interior effulgence of the lovers, sexual immersion akin to repose, power unconfined by definite boundaries. Really they are just wildlife in the garden. They strain away and toward and also try to remain still. White-coats-of-objectivity peer through one-way glass. Although science is about to name them, the lovers turn away, keeping all their tender membranes to themselves. I am visually aware of gravity's individual tug and their sensation of rising together.[15]

IF IN MIRRORS, IT DOES NOT BITE: I have seen my students absorbing postmodern tropes and reproducing them as comedy. *I took my shattered subject abroad for a term*, says one, introducing a reading, where in effect, every thing that represents 'person' is walking out of the picture. Can we do more than create narratives that acknowledge an uncanny double? It seems to me that if the job of a plot is to mirror, to create an arc or dome under which to huddle, then it is a different exercise than throwing sentences on the floor + recomposing until the door opens to something else. Just as the heavenly constellations are not visible on my dark street, not visible, in fact, because the city is itself an overlit milky way, the overdone lighting a palimpsest for the cheap electricity provided by Hydro-Québec, achieved by marching into the Cree territory of the North + turning huge rivers around to run over their electricity-producing dams. My question always, how to pursue this investigation of what will have been by opening the door in order to glimpse a more utopian future tense.

Recently a French-speaking friend pointed out to me that there is no proper future form of the verb in English. The French *j'irai*, I will go, requires, in English a compound, an additional act of will, to proceed. Grammar, the locomotion of sentences, is, among other things, a performance of the relationship between citizenship + writing subject. Living next to the elephant to the south, I have often wondered: does the citizen of a republic, occupy space—i.e., bespeak sense differently [+ by differently I do not mean better] in the 'same' English language, than, say, the subject of a former Dominion? And how does cultural hybridity—which describes an ever-increasing proportion of the Western world's population—get constructed textually? What can performance style mean if it is unclear how to speak + to whom? How many faces do you see in your mirror; in your anticipated audience? This translates into formal issues that are currently evolving with several younger writers entering the discussion. Many belong to gender minorities or write with minority languages or cultures in their immediate backgrounds, so that constant spontaneous translation is part of the writing. The epigraph to this essay from West Coast Canadian poet Rita Wong's poem "reconnaissance" describes what it means to constantly switch languages in everyday life: ...... *habitual placement of the tongue changes the mouth*... [16] ... There is so much anguish in this constant effort to perform as Other. It can also produce a sort of camp—one clearly performing a made-up wannabe version, in lieu of a so-called authentic self? To cite a Québéecoise friend: *You are nicer in French.*

THE POROUS TEXT,
OR THE ECOLOGY
OF THE SMALL SUBJECT

If the inchoate 'feminine' leaks from the *failles* of the language we are dealt to work with, still, that 'feminine' is but a part of what it means to function in the Socius beyond the walls of the Domus. Jane Austen, though constrained to work at home, knew all about that. Why else would she call a novel *Sense and Sensibility*? I won't spill ink on the debate of whether she loved a woman. Save to note a certain critical outrage at the implication, as if it tarnished her stature as germinator of rising capitalism's standard novel. Which genre has over time admirably served as a scaffold on which to hang hetero-normative romance + related social structures. Contemporary women artists often seek, because we can, utopia in the white noise of cities, the noise of crowds, of cinema, theatre, music. Noise exceeds identity; Jane would agree with that. The swirl of life cannot be reduced to a single moan.

And so I came to live a time in scintillating Paris, an ever-circulating swirl of curated illusion [clothing, buildings, bridges, perfume, picture-perfect people]. My studio, out of a Nathalie Sarraute novel, had me *on a divan. Narrow, covered with a small abstract black-and-white print. At end a rice-paper screen. Three mahogany-framed partitions. Pale eggshell walls curving gracefully at corners.*[1] Or else I wandered the streets + old arcades in search of a lost avant-garde, increasingly settling for conversation with dead Gertrude Stein + Walter Benjamin. My question to them: how does one learn to stand, as writer, as forward-looking thinker, in relation to one's own language + time? It was the 90s; in every news segment on radio/TV, the shattering racket of ethnic war—a war of mass humiliation/murder of Muslim men + mass rape of women—in Bosnia. Again, this 2020 summer, the background racket to my modest interrogation of the intricacies of language, especially as regards the negative coding of minorities, is deafening. In the current ultra-polarized context of police assassination + other misdemeanours against Black + Indigenous men + women, not to mention ongoing LGBT+ harrassment, it seems more important than ever to lend an ear to contingent majority + minority syntaxes + their implications as regards the question of power. Again I ask: who has the right to speak? To pay attention to bleeding or neighbouring syntaxes is to hone awareness—sometimes painfully, sometimes whimsically—of self-expression. Did not the great detective writer Raymond Chandler say of the [Euro-] French: *The bastards have a phrase for everything. And they are always right?*[2]

And was not I too Québécoise not to laugh at that?

//

GS + GS: The genial, the brash, the politically problematic American writer Gertrude Stein wrote in her mother English in a French-language context, as I have as well. In my case, mostly not in Paris, where Stein learned to deploy the French sentence's stress on the verb, digressing from the descriptive tendency of English phrasing. Her sentences meandered instead, gassed up on their verbs, verbs written in English but acting as if French. Long, fast, beautiful, like the American automobile she loved so much. As critic Barrett Watten has said: *Stein saw in Ford's modern poetics of repetition a mode of production that was, in explicitly literary terms, analogous to her modernist one.*[3] Both in her cars + in her sentences, she was the shiny, optimistic rover, her roving confidently reorganizing anything she touched. In her remarkable *Four Saints in Three Acts*, she made the saints the landscape. As she explained in *Lectures in America*: *All the saints that I made and I made a number of them because after all a great many pieces of things are in a landscape all these saints together made my landscape. The way they hovered over ground also made of them… blackbirds….*[4] [Or scarecrows?]

For a time, Stein eschewed commas. I had to argue with her on that. Coming from Québec to 90s Paris, I took the comma as signal of a demi-caesura: it was the comma of translation, extending one language into the space of the other. In Québec, where English persisted in bleeding into the space of the historically defeated French, to inherit the legacy of the Anglo conqueror was to be *haïe par l'histoire [hated by history]*, but [maybe] *loved by a few friends.*[5] Of course, before the [Anglo] conqueror conquered, the [Franco]-conquered also conquered. To symbolically topple—+ not for the first time—this shaky pyramid, a mixed group of Montréal militants this summer knocked down the statue of first Canadian Prime Minister John A. Macdonald, residential school founder + hangman of Métis leader Louis Riel. The current prime minister was disappointed. But for me, the constant shifting of facts in the process of translation [la Crise d'octobre does not = the October Crisis; 'femme' does not project exactly the same image as 'woman'] has fostered a perverse humour re terms like 'nation,' 'state.' Who am we? Such contrarities get into the pores when one tries to suss out a syntax that can bear the weight + music of a city. And one's relation to it. Arriving in Paris with my Anglo-Québécois accent, I quickly grasped that this accent inferred to the French a whiff of inferior, or at least provincial, culture. Some laughed outright when I spoke. I decided to laugh back. Before the end of my stay, my narrator had become a clown.

Fresh from publishing my novel *Main Brides*—a tale of inebriated lust + curiosity about certain women entering a Montréal bar—perhaps I had already, with my feminist awareness of being encoded as a smaller subject, been working on how to write my Fe-male clown. The fact of moving my writing subject closer to absorbing the warp + weave of the collective in *Main Brides* had happened by virtue of shaping the novel as installation, the drinker/narrator continually blurring, in the telling, herself + the women entering the bar. At the same time, she was, in her euphoria, elevating them, as suggests the subtitle, to float *Against Ochre Pediment and Aztec Sky*. This preceded my meeting with Stein's ephemeral landscape + blackbirds in *Four Saints*. My floating brides + their inebriated reporter were a modest attempt at distanciation, vaguely Brechtian.

I unpacked the boxed French volume of Walter Benjamin's *Arcades Project*, not yet translated into English, + placed it on the teak Paris studio desk. Read a little every day, the volume's magnificent collection of juxtaposed text-objects—thousands of carefully collected anecdotes from history books, museums, newspaper clippings, graffiti, + his personal notes—were composed into Benjamin's version of dialectic progression, where one fragment gave a new slant or questioned or opposed a preceding paragraph or fragment, without interpretive conclusion. Under rubrics from *Haussmannization* to *The Flâneur* to *The Doll/The Automaton*, Benjamin not only scored Paris as a gem of architecture + ludicrously beautiful people, he also foresaw in its visual radiance, enhanced by objects of imperial plunder, aspects of gathering global capitalism. The beauty machine was, he noted, a crucial aspect of the city's prosperity: *The clever Parisiennes.... In order to disseminate their fashions more easily...* made use of dolls: *They are the true fairies of these arcades....: the formerly world-famous Parisian dolls, which revolved on their musical socle and bore in their arms a life-sized basket out of which, at the salutation of the minor chord, a lambkin poked its curious muzzle.* [6] A few fragments later, another clipping from a journalist of the era expresses near nausea at the saccharine doll figures—even noting in disgust that the dolls, as they became worn, were given to little girls to play with.

Benjamin did not forget in this procedure of caesura + splice to continuously insert the lives of working-class men + women, their impoverishment, their uprisings. Such as this scene from the February Revolution, when one night in a wretched street of working families there was a rumble, a passing wagon:

In a cart drawn by a white horse, with a bare-armed worker holding the reins, five cadavers are arranged in horrible symmetry. Standing on the shaft is a child of the working class, sallow of complexion....; leaning backwards, this boy lights up, with the beams of his torch, the body of a young woman whose livid neck and bosom are stained with a long trail of blood... There are shouts of ... Vengeance, they are slaughtering the people.[7] His montage composition, its disjunct juxtapositions, bringing torn edges together in a new proximity served as a lesson in how to rinse sentimentalism out of writing feminism, queer, or my own biography. That is, it instructed my desire to displace the notion of individual speaking subject/agent into something more aleatory.

It amused me that in a city of faultless taste + grooming, there is no way this foreigner, with her accent, could be a 'femme' in the highly consummate French sense of the word. But as I continued the pleasurable walking, reading, + experimenting with sentences, I came through to the idea, in writing *My Paris*, to use the participle rather than the active verb in my little sentences to produce the figure I desired. For the forward agency was thus reduced, slowed to something like a passive Janus look backward, then quick glance forward. The walking figure morphing into something between 'she' + 'it.' If one says *I going down the street*, not only does the verb become mere gesture; the 'I's power is somehow reduced in the fact *of going down the street* without the help of the active verb form. And this in turn reduces the sentence to the smallest unit, extending the writing subject into its environment. What is within being intractably linked to what is without. And in all this reducing of motion + of well-fleshed narrator or character, the text + its speaker become porous. A smaller subject blends *in*, bending this way or that, depending on her interlocutor, on the assumption of what is expected of her: *Concierge ringing bell. Too early. I pretending to be up. By wearing tights to bed. Just having to throw silk shirt over.... When answering. She delivering letter. From nearly bankrupt Publisher. Saying projected little Bk. Of Murder'd Wom'n. Potential hangover. Too theoretical. Plus lacking anecdotes.*[8]

Perhaps my porous text is a guilty text. Guilty of excising the feminist heroine, for example. Guilty of creating a reticent troubled ambivalence regarding identitary issues such as gender. And as one pale of skin + gobs of Western privilege, perhaps the deep conviction of being flawed + of parading this ambivalence [in this, Jane Bowles is my sister] is to be attempting obfuscation of the worst crime of all: hypocrisy, guilt's twin!

I would protest that the Chaplinesque walking Montréaler in her little short black jacket, roomy, perhaps not impeccable, trousers, is part of an honest heritage. For the clown posture is a perpetual manifestation of being unable to live up to promise. A failure subsumed over time, starting with the unaffable bridge posture: when a minority writer, like so many anxious to please little girls, plays both ends against the middle. She may be a translator, composing language for transmigration from, say, one ethnic situation to another. For the purpose of informing the *inculte* Other. Or she is just a good woman in her womanly moderating function, explaining this, explaining that. It is a terrible posture for an artist, for it requires always reaching some conclusion, some interpretation.

The figure in *My Paris* knows, of course, that behind her small aleatory clownlike figure speaking its full-of-holes text lurks a huge shadow. The shadow of irresponsible Western culture. Her own. Speaking through her, against her. If feminism is germane to everything I have become, its perfunctoriness became an edge, at least in its 90s iteration, that I needed to exceed in order to do what I consider the artist's fundamental task: to be a critic of her entire moment, with all its contradicting vectors.

With *My Paris* came a shifting of parameters of the expression of desire. More precisely, to a posture of queer. In the moment of the 1990s, when the anti-feminist backlash was at its strongest, the notion of 'queer' seemed an umbrella term that allowed more play as far as formal issues were concerned. Although I only used the term much later, I felt less 'femme'—I was becoming 'Fe-male.' Of course, I loved that exquisite elixir that is le féminin in any language. Loved + still love it in the sense of being a part of it [only a part!], while also desiring it. But the shift was also a search for form to express not only an ongoing story of my time, but its historical underpinnings.

Gay New York prose writer Douglas A. Martin writes: *In reviews of my I-driven works, I am put to defend my use of (a) conceptual self, provisional, in a way a poet would not be....*9 This, I think, speaks to reader or critic frustration when confronted with prose sentencing that does a dance between conscious meaning + the estranging distraction of dispersed narrative or personae. Don't we all want a well-fleshed character to hang on to? Consequently, for the experimental prose writer, the answer to the surrealist question *Whom do I haunt?* may be: *No one.* This prose cannot live up to promise, the promise of what the reader wants most: to get lost in the story. Yet... *yet*......

SPACES LIKE

STAIRS

//

INTRODUCTION
[2 0 2 0]

I love the immediacy of the essay form, its way of intersecting with the period in which it is written. These essays from *Spaces Like Stairs* [1989] accompanied the writing of *Heroine* + *Main Brides*, my two most feminist novels. They resonate with a decade of remarkable flowering of feminism in Québec, a decade when the ethical function of the text was underscored in a writing practice greatly concerned with deciphering the effects of social constructs in language, especially for women. The decoding naturally left gaps in awareness. Going back to the essays, I felt a little naked. The essay, perhaps even more than fiction, shows up this youthful person radiant with hope + intractable enthusiasm. But one also pocked with her + the era's inadequacies.

Commendably, in times of continual contestation [in that sense, a time rather like now], a written text or commentary, no matter how literary, seems able to function as political intervention. Walking past the lineup of far-left groups, Maoists, Trotskyists, Anarchists, waving their newspapers in the Hall of the old UQAM building on rue de la Gauchetière, even the academy seemed breachable. At gatherings of poets, men + women around a long table, poetry's relation to politics was debated for hours. There were also meetings with feminist activists from neighbourhood + other milieus. I recall a journalist from a feminist periodical dubbing my careful intervention on fiction/theory "nothing new." I laughed! *Ex*-journalist that I was, I eschewed the sensational, that hook of the daily news, in favour of plumbing the language of received ideas. She likely laughed, too. There was nothing devastating about a good debate.

What is most progressive about these essays, I believe, is that they are not unalloyed individual performance; they come from a collective search for knowledge. It has been said that our 6-member *Théorie, un dimanche*[1] group, gathering regularly over several years to share texts on the relationship of feminist struggle to the written word, was germinal in North American feminist letters. Our intense concern as women with how we were represented in society, + in literature, allowed insights that would have been met with indifference, or even scorn, in broader contestatory contexts. We could listen to each other with utter respect; treat each other's writing with gravitas, as work of importance; pursue deeply focused investigations that liberated us from, among other things, an overdetermined deference to the authority of critical milieus + the academy.

In revising the essays for current publication, I have tried to remain consistent with the person I was then. But what to do with gaffes, unconscionable in hindsight? A militant tendency to sometimes speak in binaries has thus herein occasionally been revised or excised. As has an account, in "A Feminist at the Carnival," of crying at age 17 all the way through the grievously racializing film *Gone with the Wind*. Most probably about the love affair. I have taken out the reference, but with some hesitation: if one is to construct whiteness, ought one not openly acknowledge, rather than burying the evidence, the cruelty of the culture from which one has profited?

But mostly, the time of writing this work was a marvellous time of learning that language, lovingly, consciously used, word by word, within the space of a context, is a continuously shifting poetic project with everyday implications. Hopefully, something about these struggles for more democratic approaches to living in a community of sentences is modestly useful as we continually attempt to widen our grasp of what it means to be a fully present integral person in the broader body politic.

These selected + somewhat revisited essays from the *Women's Press* 1989 publication of *Spaces Like Stairs* appeared in turbulent times in feminist circles. I deeply appreciate Marlene Kadar's vision + editing, + the work of Rona Moreau + her *Women's Press* colleagues for making this publication possible.

VIRGINIA + COLETTE

To be a minority Anglophone in a largely French milieu in 1980s Canada surely threw more light on my own culture than on the culture of the other. In so doing, it nurtured a writer's most important task: to be a critic of one's own culture. A happy corollary: my very notion of fiction was to be transformed by the fact that my writing context happened to be distanced from the somewhat more realist fiction traditions of many English-Canadian women writers of the era. A crucial moment of that early writing education was meeting France Théoret. Our soon-intense writing relationship was abetted by shared feminism; it flourished despite the mutually antagonistic rapport that existed between our respective national cultures, in the years between the 2 independence referendums (1980/1995). When our gaze fixed on each other's culture, it often brought about amusing inversals. For example, as we grew closer, I playfully projected on her the qualities of the Euro-French Colette, a writer whom I admired far more than she did. And sometimes, I took on for her what she called the "reassuring asceticism" of Virginia Woolf. We knew these projections were absurd, but they were a way of getting behind the masks of the ethnic reticence that was an old story in both our cultures.

//

It never ceases to amaze how a concept often bears within itself its own contradiction. Example: the word 'revolution.' The 70s revolution in Poland was Catholic in part, limiting the debate on women's issues, among others, thus falling short of radical change. Marxism in its social + political manifestations has meant in several countries the right to eat versus the freedom to speak. The circus side of the Nazi phenomenon has been described as a need for ritual, pomp, ceremony, even a longing for the rites of partially suppressed Catholicism, breaking through the bland, repressive surface of German Protestantism. To be, say, Anglo or Franco as far as mother tongue contains, at its core, an attraction-repulsion attitude toward the other that is both at the root of bias + of certain *grandes passions.* The other is what we lack—or fear we lack—in self.

For women, the masculine other may be perceived as a way out of that self, amputated, refused in patriarchy; that self struggling to be a social equal. We know 'self' is something beyond the mirror image of what is played back to us as 'feminine.' But ways + means of overcoming the limits of the image can feel dangerous, because of the temptation to self-dislike, as we reject the image we see in the mirror in favour of something hopeful that stands behind it. In a gesture of transference, perhaps, I see my friend France, who hails from my immediate experience of Other, as cultural opposite. Better posture, better dress; that je ne sais quoi attributed to French women by folks of other cultures. I know I am bartering with illusion. But I must have that illusion to represent some lack I feel in myself.

France-Colette. Our meeting was prepared a long time in advance. We had grown up in the shadow of each other's culture, seduced by what we saw from afar. The discoveries we made in the process of growing closer [we met shortly after the 1976 victory of the Parti Québécois] were as much discoveries about ourselves as discoveries about the other. The confrontation of our respective versions of feminism facilitated the unmaking of respective mythologies with which we were each shouldered as female children growing up in the 50s. *If we exist anywhere,* said France, *it must be as women of our generation.* What we had in common was the social dichotomy of two women straddling a transitional epoch: Rock 'n' roll interspersed with early line-dance music was on our Saturday-night playlist. France, in a lower Laurentian town where her father had purchased a small hotel after selling the dépanneur [corner store] in St-Henri. I, in a town between Cornwall + Ottawa, where my father moved us to get away from the Air Force base.

Happiness, said Colette, *is merely a matter of changing troubles.*[1] Slightly modified, the definition could be applied to the revolving door of the identitary question. Life, like literature, is a matter of plagiarizing + cutting up. What is significant is what we choose to hear. What I hear in Colette that aids + abets me in my feminist desire to 'subvert' a devout Protestant education. That asceticism that France hears in the English Virginia. What France + I heard during the late 70s in each other's utterances, in each other's texts, in each other's approach to feminism. What we have heard that may have altered our relationship to the question of writing.

I wonder if men listen the way we have done? Colette called listening the vice that ruins the face. Our pores always open, for we were used to wanting to please others, one of the first lessons little girls learn. The beginning of *l'excentrement du je*, the decentring of self, contiguous with the repression of the little girl's libido. Her daring. Her complex desires. *C'est au fond, en petit homme, que la fillette aime sa mere*,[2] wrote psychoanalyst Luce Irigaray. But the little 'man' or little being may not have the conditions to grow up as one who exists as herself, for herself.

The product of such an education cannot but have a chancy relationship to the notion of Citizen, regardless of the language in which it is mediated. A certain cynicism starts lurking behind the face constantly striving to adapt to the reflection of itself it sees in the eye of the other. An oversensitive girl, a child of settler culture, may be acutely, if imprecisely, aware of the image she + her kind project in the eyes of an Indigenous person, for example. With what certainty she can perceive the ugliness of her own greedy 'civilization.' But what happens next? It is perhaps no accident that 2 of the white women writers most admired by Western culture [in the 1980s] grew up in white colonial circumstances: Doris Lessing + Marguerite Duras. With sensitivities that perhaps worked in both anti-imperialist + flawed perceptual ways.

Nothing gives more assurance than a mask.[3] Colette one more time. Without doubt, to adopt the posture of the writer is dangerously close to wearing a mask, to adapt early on to an image initially defined by the institutions of patriarchy. Great writer role models being still to some extent majority male. Yet the circumstances of our everyday lives make it difficult to say with the ease of a Claude Beausoleil: *Pour moi, la neige, à la limite, est plus abstraite que le texte*

[For me, snow is ultimately more abstract than text].[4] Our relationship to language, to literature, where tastes + standards are set by dominant culture, is entangled with the million little details of everyday life as 'wife,' 'lover,' 'mother.' Finding the 2-year-old's mittens, for example, gives snow a palpable edge.

To live + breathe literature, one must apparently be able to remain *au-dessus de la mêlée*—yet, ivory-tower solitude by no means implies that men through history have lived alone. A difficult life, James Joyce's, did not—despite family illness, terrible financial problems, etc.—spoil the writing. Even now, for a woman, demanding the conditions that would permit a fervent, never-ceasing relationship to *l'écriture* conjures up the image of the crochety eccentric, she who refuses the many small labours necessary for seduction, for the nurturing of other humans. Lesbians, through the sharing of nurturing, avoid this dilemma to some extent—which may explain why a good portion of the 20th century's best writing by women is by lesbians. This has not greatly enhanced society's attitudes toward women who love women.

Our discussion about how the conditions of women's lives might impact on formal issues in writing began in Québec in the mid-70s with the appearance of the feminist periodical *Les Têtes de pioche*. The air was afire with ideas, ideas that corresponded to my own struggles with writing. I was convinced, for example, that relative linear movement of plot did not correspond to the way we think, talk, live. I was looking for a relationship between my need to 'explode' language, syntax, in line with what I perceived as my fractured female being. I was also fascinated by how desire circulated through the masks that my women friends + I seemed to adopt in our various roles: mother, writer, militant, lover, friend. This seemed to preclude the development of unary female characters in prose, + consequently, of plot in any conventional sense. I was intrigued by Luce Irigaray's circular vision of things in her book *Ce sexe qui n'en est pas un*. The desire of women, she contended, does not speak the same language as that of men, but it has been covered over by male logic since the Greeks. Later this idea became, more clearly, writing across the absence that Nicole Brossard had already prophetically called *Le centre blanc*.[5]

No surprise, then, that the emphasis on language + its rapport with feminist struggle was at the core of the nurturing literary relationship between France Théoret + me. If the recurring question for us was how we stood as women vis-à-vis culture in a patriarchal society, I had a contingent question: how was this stance coloured by our respective English- + French-language [+ Protestant + Catholic] backgrounds? In her famous essay on women's writing, "The Laugh of the Medusa," Hélène Cixous talks of *female-sexed* texts: *There is not that…scission*, she says of women's writing, *made by the common man between the logic of oral speech and the logic of the text, bound as he is by his antiquated relation…to mastery. From which proceeds the lip-service which engages only the tiniest pan of the body, plus the mask.*[6]

Reading Cixous's essay was one of several factors in that heady period that dissolved any desire I had to attempt writing fiction in the usual form. Yet…*yet*…there was also the thorny problem that the feminine figure that emerged from Cixous's pages, passionately throwing her body into her speech when, for example, she addressed a public meeting, was not a fungible figure in my Anglo-Protestant education. To what extent was I different from her? Should I try to put a value judgment on that difference? Was I culturally more alienated from my physical female self than she? And what did it mean in terms of my writing? France + I began talking in earnest, often later regretting that we had failed to record our discussions. For we had embarked on a process of lifting masks, of shifting the images of self + other that were photo clichés of our respective pasts.

My first meeting with France was in a rue St-Denis café, her beret at a cocky angle, her smile friendly as she pushed her poems across the table. I was already projecting on her my image of Colette: a presence, an intelligence, both sensual + cerebral. At the same time France was probably projecting on me what she called the 'reassuring asceticism' of Virginia Woolf. But even as we reproduced in conversation our stereotypical sense of other, we mocked it. There began that strange game of mirrors, where what we thought we saw in the other was often what was trying to emerge in ourselves.

One of the notions I carry in my head of what it means to be Anglo in Québec is something akin to the Salvation Army, rigid + faintly ridiculous. Where does it come from? No doubt partly from my childhood: those endless Sunday afternoons, when Mother, who was religious, took a dim view of any Sunday activity that might be *fun*. I sat on the verandah watching the French kids across the street—with their dog Bijou, their elder sister in her high heels + makeup, their music, their laughing—watch me. Already I was aware of standing outside not only the other but also the image of self projected by the other. At the same time, I was not the figure of the young girl represented by the conventions of my own culture. France, too, who frowned at my fondness for Catholic rite, stood in a similar relationship to her culture. *The feast is hypocrisy,* she said, *the better to mask the moralism.*

For me, the masks of self + other represented by Franco + Anglo quickly gave way to that of the ideological heritage of growing up Catholic or Protestant. But admittedly, clearing that first small hurdle of nation was in itself no small matter. Not only was the weight of our respective national histories with us, but also our childhood memories of Eastern Ontario + Québec, late 50s. In the half-French village where I grew up from the age of 8, the English spoke of "the French" with disparagement, forcing on them such humiliations as the refusal of French-language high schools. Thus, the French students, unable to cope in a second language, often ended their schooling after Grade 9. For France, there was the Montréal convent where small Catholic girls were warned of the dire consequences of entering a Protestant household. I'm sure the barrier of nation was harder for France to hurdle than it was for me. She was part of a culture that was boiling with anger. But two factors, I think, made it easier: first, the 1976 victory of the *indépendantiste* Parti Québécois, an important step in reclaiming national pride, + second, the intensity of our feminism, which made us impatient to understand our past, the better to break with it.

Religion: How it, through its sometimes sly input into culture's dominant discourses, framed each of us. I remember a discussion we had about Michel Tremblay's novel *Thérèse et Pierrette á l'école des Saints-Anges*.[7] My feminism bristled at the monstrous picture Tremblay paints of the nuns. In it I saw just one more misogynist plot to put down women in Québec who had gained any access to the professions. Perhaps the rebel in me enjoyed challenging the anti-Catholic image of the sisters as punitive birds with which I was raised in our Protestant household. Where a paper pinned on the kitchen wall promised that 10 black marks for bad behaviour would mean being sent to a convent. France protests at my objections to Tremblay: *But the nuns were like that,* she says.

Still, talking to France, I insisted on the lack of female figures in Protestant iconography. Did the culmination of a long process of symbolic disembodiment of women—their erasure as symbolic body/politic incarnating another vision of life—impact social values? I became overwhelmed with the idea that English, that great language of Protestantism, had hidden, under its apparently relatively 'fair' surface, a sexism greater than any of us knew. [Danish linguist Otto Jespersen, writing in 1905, almost proudly affirms: *...there is one expression that continually comes to my mind whenever I think of the English language and compare it with others: it seems to me positively and expressly masculine, it is the language of a grown-up man and has very little childish or feminine about it.*[8]]

Could I write, then, without questioning the very matter with which I worked? As a prose writer, what would writing that was also a questioning of words + sentences in relation to each other do to the shape of a story or novel? What would it do to the reader who would have to circle back, to become involved in the process of struggling through a text, in order to work her way into some new kind of reading experience?

Which brings me back to the question of 'female-sexed' texts....French writer Philippe Sollers: *Je dirais que la reine Victoria, en chemin de fer, en train de lire un roman du XIXe siècle, c'est l'image parfaite du point zéro aù peut en arriver la littérature. Il y à la une période d'anesthésie....*[9]

It is almost a truism to say that feminist writers everywhere have struggled to express a real that has been muted with bromides tailored to the needs of a society where the *phallus* is *signifiant*. But whether there would be, in English Canada, the kind of energetic fusion between feminism + formal experiment that characterized Québec women's writing of the late 70s/80s remained to be seen. That language *was* a political issue per se in Québec was fuelled for me by the Québécois feminists I knew. In addition, we were all inspired by the language-focussed issues raised by post-May 68 writers [Roland Barthes, Jacques Derrida, Julia Kristeva, etc.] Also, in Québec, since the beginning of the modern nationalist movement, formally experimental writers such as Hubert Aquin have been a huge point of political/cultural reference.

Still, we've heard a call for female-sexed texts + something deep in us responds—though not without doubts. Maybe the call does not quite respond to needs felt by we who write in English. We have to find our *own* solutions—+ debunk our own myths. What we can learn from French-speaking feminist writers is an insistence on asserting with confidence that the feminine exsts as something culturally positive, potentially.

And what does all this have to do with the writing of prose? Plenty, I think. I see the leaves rushing along an autumnal St-Denis sidewalk. France, waiting for me in a café for what we called one of *nos dimanches durassiens*. The café feels very 'contemporary': nostalgic old-Québec decor + a certain drug trade in the washrooms. We talk of *l'écriture*, rarely of the novel or short story, or the poem. A fire crackles in the fireplace. Around us are couples, children, artists. Perhaps I notice especially the women with their bright colours, their well-groomed hair, because in our heads ring the voices, the words of other women writers. In this period where I'm reading almost nothing but women, mostly in French, + most of whom are forerunners of or bright lights of *la modernité*: Duras, Kristeva, Stein, Wittig, Brossard, Cixous, Emma Santos, Sophie Podolski [both dead, young, of suicide], Bersianik. All of them confirm what we already feel—that to express the shape of our desire, our prose must lean toward poetry [old Virginia had predicted this decades ago]. And poetry may no longer look like a poem on the page. They also confirm our doubts about sentences + the relation of subject to verb. We're listening hard to each other + scraps of our conversations end up in each other's writing. This text, for example. Or her novel, *Nous parlerons comme on écrit*.[10] Or my novel *Heroine*. One of the things we have learned in our quest is that, having for so long existed as a fiction in patriarchy, writing our own stories now is often, at least in part, a biographical process. My prose writing takes on a spiral-like movement, linked in space + time to the work of other women in Québec + elsewhere. It IS + is more exalted because it's part of a community.

This is not to deny my respect for Jane Austen, George Eliot, the Brontës. Nor for 20th century Canadian novelists like Margaret Laurence, Sheila Watson. But we are not only women living at the end of the 20th century, we are also women who—thanks to the struggles of the last several decades—are hearing ourselves in ways not heard before. Unfortunately, before being able to publish our new work expressing our subject-in-process, we have to shout down the precedents. Two of the most 'modern' of the American pre-war women writers, Gertrude Stein + Djuna Barnes, wrote out of Paris. Perhaps, still, for women writing in English, dealing with English literature is like dealing with English law. The precedents come back to haunt you. The critics remind you that the English novel in its present form was to a great extent shaped by the writing of women. So what's all the fuss? No use looking to the left for support either. Because if you fool around with the meat + potatoes of syntax + form, you have failed to take a turn to the working class, who think, we are led to believe, like white, middle-class males.

So, the process of knocking the written word into some new shape better suited to our use goes on, it seems, with increasing insistence. A community is being formed, cutting across cultures + resistances. I know my relationship with France + other Québécois women writers opened me early to work not on the whole available in English. It also led me to a new vision of my own culture, inasmuch as I could study that culture reflected in the eyes of the cultural other. Regardless of the language we speak, the culture we live in, we proceed with the double sense of both belonging + being excluded.

Montréal, 1981
Introduction revised, 2020

A VISIT TO CANADA

We both take pleasure from, + also misread each other as women from different ethnic backgrounds. Mercifully, the assumption that all women stand in the same relationship to patriarchy has been somewhat nuanced over time. In this 80s/90s moment of which I speak here, there was much cross-fertilization of ideas + mutual respect between a good number of feminists from Québec + Canada. But how much space existed for diversity of expression of women of minoritized races + cultures? Perhaps this report of travelling to English Canada from Québec in the 80s can serve as a template for the pitfalls of not stopping to really grasp the nuances of the Other. For instance, an imputation of exoticism on women of diverse minorities reveals that under the surface of our raised consciousness are buried less positive latent attitudes, vestiges of the conquest mentality of our history. Failure to hear difference between Canada + Québec women is contemporaneously less problematic than the malaise caused by failure to hear Indigenous women + other women of colour. But the experience in those early years of travelling west from Québec for literary events has been part of my learning how not hearing the Other closes space for each of us [both the speaker + the addressee]. A feminism striving for egalitarian pluralism could potentially be one of the most progressive aspects of feminist discourse. So much has changed pan-nationally since I wrote this essay. But sometimes I wonder whether what seems like increased tolerance does not gloss over the blind indifference of privilege. Certainly failure to grasp differences between women of varied European backgrounds pales compared to our failure to really 'see' women of non-Western cultures.

//

In a café on the Main, poet Erín Moure is reading me an Olga Broumas translation of an Odysseus Elytis poem. The poem is a list of nouns, sensual words from the Greek poet's place of dwelling that wash over me in a wave of pleasure…*cistern, citrus, Claire, clear sailing, cliffs, clockwork, coloured pebbles, cool wind,* etc. Words of a Greek male poet translated by a Greek-American lesbian, translated again into sound by the voice of Erín, who grew up in Alberta, reading to me, an Anglo-Québécoise, in a dark Montréal café, at a long string of tables reaching from mirrors at one end to the street at the other. The words reverberating richness in the reading/writing relationship of a work that crosses cultures, sexual boundaries, or is merely transmitted from one individual to another, each reading affected by the reader's sense of place, her sexuality, among other things.

Doubtless, in such transmissions, there is also loss. Particularly when reader/writer stand in a conflictual political or social relationship to each other. Example: the strikingly different Québécois + Canadian perceptions [readings] of the term *October Crisis* sign perpetual differing narratives in what is officially a common history. What visceral sources these different narratives seem to have, springing from a deeply emotional place when our personal, social, political cultures meet! Clearly, they comprise more than socio/political content, are a question of texture. Even an Anglophone living in Québec, provided she lives a good part of the time in French, starts to feel this difference in her body after a while.

At least, she starts to feel it on visits to the other Canada. When I travel west from Montréal, I grow aware, for instance, of feeling over-dressed. My haircuts too defined, my clothes too accessorized, my shoes too fancy. The discipline, the eye for detail in clothing, which I have absorbed from my milieu, seems in contradiction with dress, particularly in progressive milieus farther west, where dressing well seems to imply *not* sticking out in a crowd. When my brother—who lives with his 5 children in Victoria, in a sprawling stucco house complete with garden, weaving loom, + the smell of homemade bread in the kitchen—introduces me to his youngest daughter, she says: "You're joking, Daddy. That's not your sister." And I feel, sitting on his sofa in my pointed boots, my black-+-white-striped sweater, my at the moment trendy pants, cut wide at the hips + narrow at the ankles, like a misplaced dandy. The problem being that, in knowing both dress codes, one viscerally senses how each culture reads them, what's deemed attractive, + also what disturbs the eye of the beholder. So that they join, in that addendum some call inner core, almost comically, like the clashing signs of a Russian Constructivist painting.

This clashing of codes is one sign of the internal confusion that can arise from negotiating any kind of 'difference,' however small. It explains in part the temptation to play the role of *bridge*, the role of interpreter or explainer, as one's body moves from one culture to another. On visits to Canada, I am reminded that my relationship to my language + culture is also travestied in two directions in my writing. And in giving public readings or talks, I'm almost relieved that the weight of Anglo-Saxon narrative traditions remains as a kind of superego looking over my shoulder, so that I might provide the audience with some semblance of the story [I think] they want. Even if I haven't written it. While it is true that I have not experienced *le texte*,[1] that distillation of the reflexive + the literary imaginary, as palpably as my Québécoises colleagues, the endless translation of ideas from French to English in writing, in speech from English to French, also forced a certain self-reflexiveness in my fiction—not to drown in the mêlée. A doubleness much like that which women experience vis-à-vis patriarchal culture.

It was precisely to explore that gap between patriarchal culture + an emerging knowledge in-the-feminine that feminists in Québec created the genre *fiction/theory*. This was not theory about fiction, but rather a reflexive doubling back over the poetic texture of the text. Where nothing, not even the 'theory,' escapes the poetry, the internal cadence [as opposed to the internal logic] of writing. Breaking the exigencies of teleological continuity into fragments offered one means of questioning syntax/context relations. Stopping to reflect on the process within the text itself looked forward toward mutable meaning. Signified, for one, by the way Nicole Brossard uses the hologram—for a utopian reflection of woman into the future—in her novel *Picture Theory* [1982].

And fiction/theory, while it may be a method of exploring a space, a gap [without any pretension of closing it], is the antithesis of a narrative arc. What it has meant to our *La théorie, un dimanche* group, is that a woman might express her unique presence, without bowing this way + that. And once more it is important to note that the *collective* lucidity of the notion of fiction/theory was an intertextual process involving reading, talking, in which the words of other women play a key role—preparing the way for the new risks that each moves toward in her own writing.

At first [early 80s], I felt, on visits to Canada, that these new ideas from Québec were received with skepticism. Attributable to what I saw as a populist bias within progressive political culture in English-speaking Canada—a bias implying, among other things, a broad preference for 'accessibility' in art. The perception proved to be inaccurate, but clearly the terms got read differently. Trying to close the translingual gap often pushed me toward presenting overly interpretative narratives. Indeed, to be invited to speak across Canada about these issues from a Québec perspective seemed to encourage falling precisely into the role I didn't want: a go-between, a bridge from French Québec to, say, English Vancouver, or Toronto, or Windsor. A bridge that went right over my writer self, casting a shadow that left little trace of either my writing or my reflection on it. It is a mistake women often make: the habit of obliterating the self in the name of some ill-defined desire to please others. It raises the question of how for whom we imagine we write or speak alters what we write or speak. I like the French term *le rapport d'adresse*. It makes me think of fencing.

In the function of bridge or go-between, there is no equitable give-+-take. It is a function where the body of the speaker is lost in the interests of pedagogy. I felt disgruntled in this role, unsure whether I was laying it on myself or whether the growing adoration of things Québécois by some Anglo intellectuals meant that the messenger had been forgotten in the enthusiasm for the message. I did sense that people in English Canada often thought of me as having precisely the same culture as themselves. Their not sensing my efforts at translating within my own language to make my words, in part borrowed from another culture, understandable, 'accessible' to them even as I spoke, was frustrating. More importantly, I think, it reflects the arrogant assumptions of a majority culture: i.e., that a minority culture does not have the vitality to operate as a sphere of influence upon those *Others* [in this case, Québec Anglophones] who live within its parameters.

The plane to Vancouver landed in fog. In my briefcase a paper titled "Body/Language/Text." It started by making a point about the relationship between body, text, with a reference to the French writer Barthes.... *Summing up his likes and dislikes, Barthes says he likes salad, cinammon, cheese, marzipan, etc. He doesn't like white Pomeranians, women in slacks (sic), geraniums, strawberries, the harpsichord, etc. All this proves, he concludes, is that his body is different from anyone else's....* 2

To start with Barthes was to justify what I feared might otherwise be regarded as 'essentialist' by [post]-modernists in the audience. If for Barthes, small things like tastes in food could be considered part of a larger inscription signifying a body's distinctiveness, could one not leap to saying one's writing might be impacted in the process of inscription by one's [conscious or unconscious?] reading of the gendered body guiding the pen? Ironically, to make my point about how gender might affect one's relationship to language, I invoked Luce Irigaray's radically poignant +, in fact, much criticized 'essentialism'; I liked her way of asserting the connection between a woman speaking + the movements, rhythms of her body, particularly as regards her sexuality.[3] I am aware of the dangers of speculating, as regards the impact of gender on speech + especially on writing. But how to separate the effect of one's biology [+ sexual orientation] on one's relationship to language from the impact of other types of social conditioning, such as race + class? How to keep all of them to the fore at the same time without suppressing one or the other +, in the process, the integral speaking subject?

On that trip to Vancouver, my decision to play a role of transmitter or bridge meant that only part of my narrative could be visible. The texts of the Québécois women about whom I was talking had been involved in a weaving, had been intertextual to my work; but my work had also been absorbed into that of the others in our little group in the previous five years. And this I had buried in the interests of being the 'Québec expert.' As Nicole Brossard put it:

The private is political, I improvise on new ground. I take back my rights, what is due me.... Words surface, coming from afar.... I exhibit me for us, that which resembles us. I write and I don't want to do it alone... [4]

I loved Louky Bersianik's relentless efforts to get beyond syntax's refusal of the female subject, which she saw as a collective project. *Something hasn't happened that should have happened. The image-attic has been pillaged, havoc has been wreaked in the memory box. All that's left is the somebody says; the what-would-they-says; all that's left is the water sprites, the shock waves of the shimmering ripples of a single facet of memory, its ticklish unglorious part. All that remains, monstrously, is women's amnesia.... Will we or will we not,* continues Louky in her wonderful text *Les agénésies du vieux monde, enumerate and analyze all existence to try and separate out that which belongs to us, to rediscover ourselves?* 5

Significantly, at the end of my talk, a lovely woman in the audience said: "Very interesting, but I would have liked to hear more about you."

Of course she was right. To establish a veritable give-+-take dialogue, I needed to share my own work, rather than suppressing it in favour of the bridge function. What is lost is the possibility for a greater *rapport d'adresse* between writer + audience when a text is nourished by + written in one cultural context, + published + read in another? My texts leave Québec, where they are read in [French] translation by my Québécois peers, to visit Canada, where they are read in English. And certainly some Canadian readers, without thinking, because naturally living in the house of their own language, expected my work to have a direct kinship with the social + formal concerns raised in their community.

This gap between the culture of the reading community + that of the community from which the text is written affects the text even on the level of syntax. The writer, in constantly taking wild leaps over those cultural gaps, is a Janus head, looking in two directions, an exercise both fascinating + disarraying in its implications. Until she realizes she has no choice but to try, in her writing process, to leave spaces into which the other, the reader, can read her own difference. So that each difference may be confronted, felt within the text.

Everywhere are assumptions of sameness to be challenged. A text, for example, carrying an unacknowledged cultural difference in the country called Canada can't help but implicitly challenge certain assumptions about language [+ about Canadian history] held by so many, for whom the relationship to language is not, historically, one of oppression. Sometimes when I read criticism of my work coming from English Canada, I have to translate the criticism. By that I mean I have to guess where the critic is writing from, guess at its subtext coming from its community fabric, in order to understand it. Just as s/he has speculated, given the necessary loss of nuance, in reading. How much more frustrating + infuriating must this situation be for women whose cultures are non-European?

Yet, for my part, these 'visits' to Canada, a little complex + painful, have also been warming. The awareness of, the space for, language + cultural differences [+ likenesses] between Québécois women + Anglo-Canadian women has opened considerably in recent years. Now, are we white feminists capable of leaving open, in our hearing of racial, ethnic, regional differences, the space for the integral other that we have claimed for ourselves in our discourse on, among others, *new writing in-the-feminine?* In this, hopefully, we have gained some understanding + solidarity, despite our differences, vis-à-vis patriarchal culture. The more we grasp that in a sense all of us have a double, perhaps multiple, relationship towards the culture(s) that surround(s) us, the more we will be able to acknowledge differences, oppressions, hierarchies, among women. And the more we will be able to stop some of the loss of translation.

Sitting in that café on the Main listening to the voice of a poet, a lesbian, reading me a poet from another [European] country, another alphabet, whom she loves, translated by yet another poet, Olga Broumas, Greek as the poet Odysseus Elytis is Greek, yet, also, a woman like us, I think: This is a safe translation. Somehow, here, has been established a string of equalities that transforms

possible loss [there is inevitably loss] into wealth. The energies—
the cultures bouncing off one another in the café whose tables are
lined up like a string of inverse mirror images—headed toward
the energy of the street.

Montréal, 1986, 1988
Revised, 2020

A STORY BETWEEN
TWO CHAIRS

We have made modernity too subservient to objective parameters.
Modernity is also related to the art of writing and to life.
—poet Normand de Bellefeuille, at "Vouloir la fiction,"
[*la nouvelle barre du jour* colloquium, 1984]

The astonishing influence feminist writers had, in the late 70s/80s, on contemporary writing in Québec is reflected in this citation from Normand de Bellefeuille. A key figure of Québécois modernity, de Bellefeuille is speaking here of a relationship of desire between writing, body, life, + a more abstract notion of 'text' as…a web of signfication + an intertexuality that has no origin nor destination. *Several feminist writers attending the 1984 "Vouloir la fiction" colloquium in Montréal saw themselves as operating on this cusp between post-structural abstraction + a need to express whatever is meant by 'the feminine.' Organized by the periodical* la nouvelle barre du jour, *the colloquium, attended by male + female poets, was essentially a discussion on the fate of* la modernité *in the 80s. There was some tension between feminists, with their* nouvelle écriture, *+ their male post-modern allies, on one hand, + a small group of writers who said they were fed up with modernist inhibitions.*

The 'fiction' wished for or desired in the naming of this colloquium was that of a textual practice that allowed for a 'theoretical imagination.' And, yes, women writers were at the forefront in these matters. But it WAS 1984, + the literary avant-garde was suffering from the same temptation as the political avant-garde à few years earlier: the temptation to step out, however briefly, from what sometimes seemed like an overly ascetic marginality. Some of us had novels in our drawers. Personal essays were being considered…. Was the text, that form so treasured by Barthes + other post–May '68 theorists, about to be swallowed by a new reformism?

//

Fiction 1984. A woman sitting in a corridor. Trying to avoid the sounds of war. Cacophony of clichés. Does *fiction* mean *une création de l'imagination (Larousse)* or is it *fictitious literature, esp. the novel or short story (Webster)*? I know. Compromise. Adopt a hybrid. How feminine! Weave what's gapped into. Pretext. Woman, in corridor. Outside the sounds of war. Trying to avoid cliché, she writes. Listening to the animal inside her. Trying to fix a line between the music of voices, her women friends, + god. The Father. What coding then applicable? Pluralism? Social revolution? Feminism? No discourse is pure. Just women sitting in a corridor. All the world a stage, the men. She writes, an other language. So stay guilty! An inverted reflection gives an extremely theatrical perception. Self as… pale

Amazon. Perversely drawn by the lure of negativity. She writes. For whom? Outside the sounds of war. She writes. Identity needs appearances. Story. A little order in decaying century. The holes show. Never mind. Under the surface, some useful fragments. But who can speak of that? The family's back....

A portion of the colloquium proceedings was published in *la nouvelle barre du jour* alongside our texts...

"What do you mean by listening to the animal inside her?" one of the writers asked. I had to admit I meant listening to something essentially feminine, to a part of self-as-woman not quite integrated into the law, perhaps closer to 'nature.' In modernist terms, this was heresy. But hidden behind that animal inside lay a real difference between feminist writing practice + that of non-feminists identifying with literary modernity. For the modernist desire to disperse the writing 'I' across an experimental space unfortunately too often got articulated as if every text were written from the same universal locus: male, white, educated. Whereas feminists interested in modernity saw a problem with the assumed universality of the writing subject [+ the degree of its author-ity in relationship to the writing]. If the desire was to create a new female subject-in-process through the act of writing, it was also, in fact, a process of deconstructing traditional fictions about women. I knew the animal inside me was a reflection of something else, a wish, a dream. But could a woman write without this dream, this imagining of a no longer indiscible?

On the other hand, I was also starting to feel uncomfortable with the restrictive way 'feminism' sometimes got applied to writing practice: the rigid attitudes prevailing in certain milieus about what a 'feminist heroine' is, for example. If writing is the act of always seeking more understanding, more lucidity, prescriptive directives have no place in our trajectory toward the delightfully mysterious edge of language. I said, in answer to a question on that issue, "Feminism is a way of life for me. But when I write I feel I can be confident my feminism is a given without having to check constantly if my text is 'correct.' ... *In other words, I trust that my political consciousness is part + parcel of my personal integrity, hence of my way of thinking. But I will not let it play the role of superego.*

I was also asked what I meant by "pale Amazon, perversely drawn by the lure of negativity." *My reply:* To be Anglophone in Québec can be to wear a history which renders one guilty, which diminishes the self-image of the politically sensitive person. *When you find yourself in this conundrum + at the same time, feel a tremendous solidarity with what has been going on in the way of Québécois affirmation in the twenty years leading up to the 1980 referendum, the positive, upbeat image often expected of feminist fiction seems oversimplified.* It's one of the reasons I'm often tempted in my writing to inverse things, usually ironically, to the dark side of the paradigm.

Montréal, 1984

PARAGRAPHS BLOWING
ON A LINE

ENTRY 1

This diary was written over the years I worked on my novel *Heroine*.
A diary that has been condensed, entries altered, renumbered:
a fake diary in a sense. Written often in a café with a blue floor,
where, for a while on the café wall, hung the perfect iconography
for a woman struggling with the novel form: a poster of a sailor
with a drawn knife standing under the tower of Pisa—which had
become a *precariously leaning penis*.

ENTRY 2

When I think 'novel,' the images flood in on me from the exterior (the city); from memory, too. I can't believe their richness:
the street images deeply musical. The heroine washed over by
the poetry—and the voraciousness—of the city. I write, but I'm

writing round in circles. Often uncut by periods (sentences). I love this poetic confrontation with language. But the novel requires some attempt at making sense. Some forward movement, presumably encapsulated in grammatical units of time represented by the sentence. Is not a novel above all a recording of moving (changing) time?

ENTRY 4

My character: a woman in a bath. She's oblivious, for she's masturbating under a jet of water. I have to find a narrative way to give her meaning. Some plot to tie together the memories floating past her in the steam, not only the lost love, but also the dissolution of certain political dreams in what she knows already will be the 'Yuppie' decade (the 80s). And, to relate these somehow to the images from the 'exterior,' the street. Such as that domed-shaped café and women in cloche-shaped hats because the ambience is 30s, Berlin in the air [time's strange repetition propensity]. Fragments of her best friend, Marie, in her apartment, dropping pot on the floor + saying (because she is order where the main character is chaos): "je ferai le ménage demain." Her repugnance of disorder a legacy of generations of Québécois women ordering the chaos of colonization.

A bell in my head says, Produce, produce. But I can't just sit down + write a novel about X. It all happens in the process of writing. As Barthes mentioned: writing has to do with the body's pursuing *its own ideas—for my body does not have the same ideas I do.*[1]

ENTRY 5

Both the self-reflexive and the 'poetic voice' implied by the present tense appear to close some of the space between writer and text.

Poets generally feel no need to hide behind fictional characters. With fiction, it's different. Even so, people will say "it's autobiography, like all first novels." Odd how many women keep writing 'first novels' over and over again. In Québec, we've been saying that women, in writing their own gendered voices, are creating a real that has to date existed only as fiction created by males.

ENTRY 6

It's a bright crisp winter day. I keep writing, writing, but can't get past those first pages that came to me as a song in the blue café the other day. The music of the words balancing her guilt, her dilettantism. She's a 'revolutionary' but also the petty bourgeois, the imperfect feminist + the badly loved woman—although she doesn't see that at first. Still, she has her ideals, which I'll have to work on a little. Now I find it impossible to recapture the way the sentences swing between past and present, between 'inner' and 'outer.' The beauty of her nostalgia is transformed to a heavy sadness that doesn't satisfy me at all.

ENTRY 7

What dissatisfies me about her sadness is that she can't just be lying in the tub lamenting her problems (even love, as she sees it, is a 'luxury' compared to what many less-privileged women are experiencing). There would be no point in adopting the novel form if I were not aiming to reflect both her interior world and the 'universal' questions of an epoch. For example, the issue of revolutionary social change—incarnated by the events in Poland (late 70s)—might show how slant the issue of revolutionary purity appeared to the women comrades of the left group she joined. For in Poland the Solidarity movement, which the male comrades hoped would lead to a new type of revolution within the socialist state, remained Catholic + patriarchal.

Again, the issue is form. The left has long held up Brecht as a solution. It's true, the Brechtian model was greatly ahead of the direct representation model of social realism in the way his characters become analogies of social problems—Mother Courage, for example.

But what to do with this very unfeminist idea my heroine seems to have that the past always seems best?

ENTRY 8

On the wall of the blue café, a huge poster advertising the Chantal Akerman film *Toute une nuit*. A woman in a midnight-blue dress, 40s-style, high heels. Walking the streets of a Belgian city with other women + their men, almost wordlessly (the film has very little dialogue). Yet—becoming a social commentary on middle-class sex roles, while leaving the spaces (due to the silences?) for the viewer to feel, imagine, the inner thoughts of these women. So that the viewer participates in closing the gap between women's inner + outer experience.

If only I could find a way to do this in words, to make possible a reading other than the one necessarily arising from the author's being stuck—as I am—in the writer/narrator/novel subject relationship. It's her voice I want to explore, rather than being out there in culture looking down on her.

Meanwhile, I'm failing to relate to my poor secondary characters. One is a Black man looking through a telescope on the mountain. I have no idea who he is or what he is doing there. And the grey woman, who has come over from an older unpublished manuscript. Then there is this person my heroine addresses in moments of great excitement, called Sepia. Who or what is Sepia? Memory perhaps, but coloured like an old photo, the sepia tint taking away the sharp contrast between black and white. There is something dreamlike about this Sepia. She seems to represent an ideal of perfection. The moment of 'love' in a Northern European town that my heroine recalls, mooning over a photo taken of her + her ex-lover. The photo lies now on a stool by her tub.

ENTRY 9

No one would dare call *The Sorrows of Young Werther* melodrama. Yet imagine a woman trying to write a story of such...hysterical obsession with the love object. A love so unbearable, young Werther had to kill himself.

It's a fact that there's something a little off about my heroine's relationship to this...melodrama. What if she is only participating in it as a way to cope? We all have memories of participating in various not-quite-appropriate narratives, the better to live up to an image projected on us from outside. Maybe melodrama is another form of fake narrative to carry one through difficulty.

Like in the soaps, my heroine's story might involve an almost theatrical repetition of emotions. Maybe using a repetitive image, like Proust's bell ringing when Swann enters the garden gate, to give a critical distance to the 'story.'

The whole novel could proceed as a series of her bird's-eye views from the bathtub. This would be a way of integrating different times, levels of consciousness: her nostalgia, vs. commentary produced by the narrator's feminist consciousness. Except I want this to be exploration, not prescriptive writing. All language has to be seen as material to work on.

ENTRY 12

People are lined up for the cinema at the back of the blue café to see Werner Schroeter's *Répétition générale*. It's a film about an alternative theatre festival at Nancy, brilliantly and subversively combining various genres. Example, using documentary images from the carnival of plays as a commentary on our times, as well as interjecting a bit of the director's autobiographical commentary, a bit of a love story that might be his personal fiction, and even Prometheus on a roof providing a deconstructed mythological angle on the whole thing. I envy people who work with visual images (performance artists, filmmakers, installation artists). The audience seems to accept that visual images can slip, may have multiple meanings, whereas writers, especially those working in prose, can easily be trapped in the preconceived notions ascribed to words by ideology.

ENTRY 13

A compromise might be possible: structuring the story by means of the fluctuations in her…(dare I?) hysterical voice. The use of the voice invoking a poetic meaning in excess of the sentence. But the forward movement of the healing process, i.e., her coming-to-awareness of what needs to be changed, displaced in her context in order to come through the labyrinth, invoking the novel. The opening scenes of her in the bath are very mad, for she's remembering it all at once. Then relative calm: her (bath) mood altered by remembering moments of euphoria. This plot, the plot of her obsession, dealt with *blow by blow*.

But it's clearly only a thread of the whole: the memory of each scene is framed by her attempts in the tub to create a 'present.' Juxtaposing the woman from the past (memories, perhaps recorded in a diary) in relation to the 'now' woman, she who is commenting on the situation of disintegrating advanced capitalism, which keeps reviving like a spent prick, conjuncturally featuring as its great achievement in personal relations: the royal couple + its apex of creation: the nuclear family.

And I just wrote that the relationship can be dealt with *blow by blow*. Blows: violent + unusual interruptions in her narrative texture—which texture the writing is hopefully starting to discover. More + more, I intuit that it has to do with starting from a negative point: a crushed ego that doesn't see its boundaries. Except who ever heard of a novel hero/ine with a crushed ego? You might say Proust's or Kafka's heroes—yet little Marcel, has, at least, despite his insecurities, an intricate sense of self. Another problem: *écrire un roman, c'est se constituer comme sujet...* (Québécois writer Lise Gauvin).

ENTRY 14

Milan Kundera: The novel is an interrogative meditation of experience. *Whose* experience? But I am not proposing the opposite of that cool meditation either—even if my promiscuous relationship with my narrator still risks being too sticky.

If I were a painter, I could get the charge of subjectivity right, painting over it until it became 'art' at the same time as I caressed it (her). As in the succinctly brushed watercolours of Virginia Woolf, or Jane Bowles's bright bits of colour floating chaotically in the clear air, or Djuna Barnes' black with the odd bits of circus red, or the shadowlessness of Nicole Brossard's writing (is it the absence of the past for her that makes her writing *sans ombres*, as F.T. says?). In fact, I imagine this novel's sepia tint of a photograph having occasional touches of colour—like when you paint on a black-and-white photo. The colour being the immediacy of her commentary, of what she wilfully adds to the image to make it hers, to make it radically different from *his* image. That shot of them leaning together in the Northern European courtyard, for example. The trick being to find the potentially moving point (Barthes' punctum) in the 'still lifes' taken by him that are on the stool by her tub. The point that draws her perception beyond his framing of the image into a new story. She's working from a negative (reading) of these images, images she will take off + arrange her own way. At first his black-+-white images are what she wanted to climb into. Where she fled obsessively—for comfort.

ENTRY 15

If I were to hang my 'negatives' on the line in a new chapter order, it would be:

1. Sepia (the café on the Main with him sitting under a bleeding loaf of bread).
2. The Dream Layer (*l'étreinte* in the Northern European courtyard).
3. Euphoria + the New Order of the Revolutionary Couple (a scene from their apartment).
4. The Resentment (she tries to escape into art).
5. Feminism (she leaves the revolutionary organization in a long skirt).
6. The Rupture (the last wait on the balcony).
7. Under the Line of Pain.

But it's odd how one can't will order even by writing it down. For Under the Line of Pain is *not* chapter 7. It's there all the time, through her whole night of remembering "what happened." It is vexing that certain feminists prefer to deny the pain, glossing over it. Have they forgotten Barnes' terror of abandonment? Woolf's terror of schizophrenia? Jane Bowles ordering whisky after whisky until she collapses in Montréal Central Station….

ENTRY 16

At the next table someone is telling a story about a woman lawyer, a brilliant criminal lawyer who fell in love with one of her criminal clients + ended up following him to a foreign country. There he treated her…criminally. Finally she came back, her professional credibility destroyed. Then her mother, whom she dearly loved, died. She spent months wrapped in her mother's things, rocking in her mother's chair.

I can't resist the texture offered by a voice like hers. I imagine it swinging from a poetic excess of words, context, to a feigned control (deferring to some sort of borrowed narrative). The latter with an apparently smooth surface, but with such spaces between the words as to imply another meaning. This is the real meaning of writing over the top: the text, the writing, becomes a kind of third voice, not the author or the narrator, but the voice of the author/narrator subsumed—as opposed to commenting from a traditional narrative distance—into the object of narration. Jane Bowles writes brilliantly in this third voice. She's found a way to leave behind the univocal author, so that the writing subject exists at the point where the inner + outer voices meet. Instead of a distantiated reading, you get a maddening buzzing effect.

ENTRY 17

What is the present, anyway, but a defence against memory? Or rather, a defence against nostalgia: the narrator has to defend herself against the character she has created for whom *the past always seems best*. It is ironic that despite the fuzzing of the narrator's boundaries with those of the author, in terms of what she thinks, I shall clearly, wilfully, invent this narrator as I go along. The invention must be the result of her movement through language, though, + not the inverse. To do this is to assume that what she thinks is important. And this assumption + this invention are my real concessions to the novel form.

ENTRY 18

In the blue café. Bessie Smith is singing *Nobody Cares For Me*. Reminding me that the song form seems closest to the voice/body proximity I want to evoke in my writing. The novel a jazz counterpoint with all those notes floating around in the air, every so often you pick out a melody to help it 'move forward' a little. Catching what you catch.

In fact, the heroine has a present/absent bodily relationship to context. The streets are a spectacle her body takes in. The female body, fragmented, its cells reaching out to all the other fragmented, pained bodies, the women, the poor, the effects of *les restes de la colonization*, is sometimes literally splayed over the city. Bodies talking.

ENTRY 21

I think I'm finding a form to permit me to write what Carla Harryman calls the middle ground…*where what's enlarged (subjective) and what's reduced (external) by speaking gather*.[2] At least inasmuch as I manage to protect the voice of the text from bending to a desire to interpret.

Could this character, so birdlike, infinitely poetic, beautiful, chaotic…+ ultimately, wise…emerge as anything but an artist? Her voice pitched in a tone of *Je ne regrette rien*. In constant movement from one café to another, from place to place. Between the 'phallic battering' of a society stacked against women, + her labyrinthine voyage through memory + the present. *More easily rendered in a sonata than in a novel*, to quote the tub-woman.

ENTRY 24

In the blue café, really called Café Méliès, after the founder of the French cinema, a lover of the fantastical… Trying to write quite a long passage now on the warmest period, the period of great complicity among women. That high watermark of feminism (late 70s) when the restaurants for the first time were full of women in pairs, in groups. When one was experimenting, at last, with trusting women first. And the ambiguous sexuality in the air, the fading of the line between lesbian + straight. This is the period in the novel, in her remembering, where she 'writes over the top' quite easily, as if from a new ethic.

In the projection room at the back of the café, they are showing Cocteau's *Orpheus*. The woman in it reminds her of her best friend Marie, with her 40s-style nipped-in waist + black gloves. Marie is the best kind of feminist, committed, yet capable of facing the inevitable.

ENTRY 25

It's true: the need to accomplish this thing—which is both to posit some new kind of subject + to have the sense of being a subject myself—requires creating a feminist *ligne directrice*—what Barthes calls…the staging of a new 'father,' a new hierarchy of acceptable concepts. (*Every narrative (every unveiling of the truth) is a staging of the…father.*) Maybe what my heroine discovers in trying to write her novel is only that the novel doesn't suit a (diffuse?) way of seeing things. Where there is closure (firm conclusions) in many novels, there are spaces, questions in hers. Even her anecdotes point to other possible representations.

Still, given that my firm + conscious intention has been to counter (patriarchal) ideology in this process, the post-structuralist recipe for taking apart everything from the sentence to the author won't entirely do. I have to at least propose some other direction, given that language slips all around us. One's response to that is a question of the relationship between writing (what it comprises of consciousness) + body. Again to quote Barthes: *The text needs its shadow. This shadow is a bit of ideology, a bit of representation, a bit of subject: ghosts, pockets, traces, necessary clouds. Subversion must produce its own chiaroscuro.*[3]

ENTRY 26

The Black tourist also walks through the city with a broader view of seasons, life, etc. The tub-talk, which frames the nostalgia, operates then within the larger frame of the Black man's telescope at the mountain lookout. Alternately, at the street level frame of the city, with the grey woman going through it. This double framing means the scenes are separated by spaces, quite big ones, as if spit forth from a snowstorm. Spaces where, hopefully, interesting things might happen in the reader's mind. Spaces also offering an almost overdetermined means of separating me the author from the narrator Gail. Indeed, the Black man on the mountain, looking through the telescope, is creating his own order. She can't hear his thoughts. Nor those of the grey woman, who hardly speaks, except in nonsensical rhymes. But the grey woman calls up in her the desire to get out of it all, regardless of where that desire will take her. This temptation of utter solitude is reinforced by the heroine's feeling she's safe with nobody. And you can't survive in this society with nobody. *Jeanne Gilmore, a 33-year-old homeless woman, was found dead outside a hot air vent this morning. The temperature had dropped to 30 below overnight.*

ENTRY 27

And now I have to end this somewhere. Sitting in the blue café the other day, with a toothless, hungry woman outside the window, I had this idea (quickly discarded) that the story would end with my heroine sitting between two homeless women on the Main. A passerby would say to one of them: "your cunt smells." And she (an ex-hippie) would reply, laughing toothlessly: "I can't wash it, I've got a Molotov cocktail between my legs."

ENTRY 28

Some novelists claim their characters come to them like other voices. I'd have to say that it is, rather, the structure, that offers itself as a revelation as a work is finishing. Of course, it doesn't "come to me" but is the fruit of my own hard thinking, + a considerable process of intertextuality, especially with other women's work. In fact, I am learning to trust my feminist consciousness enough to forget it when I write. It is there partly as ballast, but ballast that by moments must be left behind, risked, in order to reconnoitre. A heroine has to finally face her grief, uncensored. To really read her diary about those years when she felt dominated by feelings of victimization, anxiety. To stop repressing the writing, which is the only possibility of leaving a trace (a fleeting 'presence' is better than none).

Yes, she will read her diary, deciding to use the writing in it as material, cut up collage-style, for the novel. She will get out of the tub + enter the city, thinking about these things. Walking through an early winter street, she will think of these things + of the women she may see, meet. And she will think of who/where she will be next. There will be no revelation, no blinding light on the road to Damascus. Just her walking through the snow. The novel will end with

She—

Montréal, 1982–86
Revised, 1988
Excerpted, 2020

A FEMINIST AT
THE CARNIVAL

This essay has been published over + over, in English, in French, + back.
This version is a combo of the original + of the one included in co-publi-
cation with my Theory, A Sunday *cohorts (2013).*[1]

QU'EST-CE QUI EST INCONTOURNABLE [Eng. trans: unskirtable!] dans le féminisme quand on écrit? I love that, the idea of
one's feminist consciousness being **unskirtable**, i.e., untameable,
unladylike… What of one's feminist consciousness is unskirtable
in writing? 'Honesty' comes my somewhat incongruous + intellectually unsatisfying answer. Does that mean one's feminist consciousness keeps one honest? Or does it mean the opposite: that
one's writing somehow transcends one's political commitment?
'Honesty,' I answer stubbornly, while in my mind, the feminist who
wants positive, forward-looking models for women confronts

the writer who envies Proust + Kafka. What does she envy? Their 'freedom' to follow, in their fiction, the darker trails of being. Fittingly, outside it is a grey November day. Through my rue Jeanne-Mance window, a suite of 3-dimensional planes. The bare trees in the immediate foreground. Across the street, the rounded garrets, the fancy trim on top of turn-of-century houses. Behind them a high-rise building blocking a portion of the sky. And to the left of that, tucked in a corner of the picture, the hump of mountain with its cross. That cross—shining absurdly bright up there as if melodramatically overstating a much-diminished power.

Arbitrarily, I choose this setting for my heroine. She's a writer who wants to explore the uncanny, maybe even delve into women's tragic potential. Except the word 'tragic,' when traced (indirectly, on her computer screen), glitters with irony. Did not classical tragedy's cause-+-effect narrative underscore patriarchal values? Aspiring to singular, larger-than-life heroes who wouldn't reflect her sense of self? True, *elle a envie de vivre grande*, to cast shadows like Ozymandias on the sand. But...a female-sexed Oedipus? Absurd. A feminine Hamlet? Closer, maybe. Still, there's something unsuitable (for her) about his relationship with his mother...

Yet it's precisely toward those figures she feels herself reaching. Reaching for something beyond the almost too-perfect 'strong women' of certain feminist novels, marching with their sisters toward an idealized future. Reaching, of course, also beyond that other extreme of women's fiction: the soapy heteronormative novel obsessed with risks + perils of heterosexual love. True, the cry for love compels her, being 'tragic' for she who's devastated by it, but melodramatic for arbitors of literary culture. Reaching, too, beyond the sensationalist factoids expressed in the journalese of newspapers: *tragic* poverty; *tragic* accident; *tragic* rape + murder.

She recognizes them as surface signs of some deeper riddle in-the-feminine lurking in the human psyche; as some remote error of a civilization that refuses to confront death—while wreaking it on the balance of the planet.

Defiantly, she reaches toward the unspoken, because to do so is the ultimate proof her own women's culture has come of age enough to trust her when she writes. But in that space beneath the mantle of courage, of bravery that women have worn for centuries, she'll find what?

1. In old movies, the tragic moment was often signalled by clouds amassing in the sky. Driving along the highway with huge black moving clouds banking before the storm, one gets a terrible feeling of human emptiness. The mind casts about desperately for the source of discomfort. It may fasten on fear of an accident as the big raindrops start. As they begin hitting the windshield with greater and greater force. No, the mind knows this fear of an accident is really a projection of fear from a deeper source: fear of the uncanny. In a jigsaw puzzle, you take apart the clouds gathering angrily over the spacious park above the castle. AND YOU FIND NOTHING. This is both reassuring and terrifying.

2. Sitting, as a girl, on the verandah in the village where I grew up, I was drawn by the angry pink-black clouds. Beside me, mosquitoes bit at my brother's neck, causing huge red welts. I was glad. I hated him. He was my Mother's favourite. I watched the storm whipping up the dust by the side of the road. Mother was standing behind my rocking chair. Her unhappiness was the

turmoil in all our souls. Beyond our lawn, other dramas with no solution were being played out in our half Irish Protestant, half French village with its red-brick houses and false-fronted stores.

But here the narrator senses a dichotomy. On one hand she understands (grasps with her whole body) the need for the positive reaffirmation of a more or less universal female subject. In fact, she remembers exactly the moment she grasping this completely. Summer 1977, in Montréal. Women on a lawn, drinking sparkling wine. Their soft voices, their soft hair, seeming to waft through the air. One of them had written: *Women in space*. Meaning, of course, not women astronauts. But women occupying space, now at last, as it spirals out before them. On some crazy, wild, maybe above all erotic voyage to the future.

On the other hand, there was the little girl, the little Fury, sitting there with her mother behind her, watching another mosquito expertly dig its long, delicious point into the white neck of her brother. The first heavy raindrops made the dust on the road bounce up in lacy little circles. She hardly knew what *tragic* meant, but something drew her toward that dark place the word would come to represent.

Later, her empathies were more tangible: her friends, a single mother with several children down the street, the war-torn migrant women from Vietnam, then Chile, + of course, feminists everywhere.... Still, she noted in a green notebook with white tulips embossed on the cover:

Woman has a narcissistic, almost masturbatory image of love
The image of the beloved is more precious than his presence

It was the morning after a love affair, + she was watching herself. Watching like the little Fury had watched [herself] watching her brother. That watched self becoming, then watching, other selves: the self that's critical, for example, of certain other women; or of she who has just written in the new notebook in the café of a museum. The watched selves opening out infinitely like a Russian doll. Or like the hieroglyphics of the Russian futurist painter Popova, climbing in crooked lines across her work as if a score for urban music. To the left of a scene stands Stalin like a magnanimous cuckold.

In the museum café, my heroine added to her notes in the green book:

Mon Heroine a envie de vivre grande.
That is where transgression starts.

Sensing also the gap between her grandiose desires + the nagging pang inside—that covered what?

Here's the rub: a contemporary feminist heroine's meant to be a model of progress. While Oedipus, apparently, was a loser: struck by Fate for killing Dad, the better to sleep with Mother. As for Hamlet, he lost [his sense of self, allegedly] because he couldn't choose between his mother + his father. His *To be or not to be* was a contemplation of suicide issuing from the depths of his existential despair [that hidden fear that he was homosexual?].

A female heroine uttering the same phrase would more likely be contemplating everyday life. Her question being *To exist or not to exist* as speaking subject? A question to which a writer who's a feminist can only answer in the positive. *To be.* For to answer otherwise would be to shrink back into the chaotic space of non-subject, into the clichés that have often objectified her in the culture.

In women's novels of the 70s + early 80s, *To be* has been to kick + scrape our way out of the margins of patriarchy [the kitchen, the wife of the traditional heterosexual couple], ascending or side-stepping into historical space. Except, as Virginia Woolf already warned in *Three Guineas*, stepping into male *processions* [the professions of law, politics, academia, for example] was dangerous because it had to be on male terms. So that *To be*, as woman, a subject in all her articulated difference, where her gestures might really match her words, could never be completely satisfied.

Another space of 'being' in women's fiction is the Amazon utopia. This space, *unconditionally lesbian*, avoids the dilemma raised by Woolf—of trying to make it on patriarchal terms—by locating herself, at very least in her personal life, beyond history. In a space where she, the future-projecting Amazon, becomes... a new icon. But *utopia is an emotion*,[2] not necessarily psychologically accessible to every writer. And my heroine, who's trying to create other heroines on her computer screen, also sees the Amazon [although admittedly attracted to her] as a self-proclaimed superior. As if the Amazon, in rising to her utopia, casts shadows not only on the ground, but also on other women.

Where, then, + *how*, might my subject, denied her full existence in any patriarchal paradigm, yet not seeing herself as 'Amazon,' be a subject-in-the-feminine? That is: where + how in writing? If she [who on the computer screen still appears in series, all the watched parts constantly coming apart, fitting together again...] cannot be expressed in any established form, she needs to find another place where the words she speaks will fit her gestures. A place as excessive as the Amazon's bold step outside history, yet—she's a Capricorn—a place where her struggle for integrity might be more earthbound than the Amazon's utopia.

The heroine smiles. Maybe the Dark is just utopia inside out. Maybe the basic characteristic of writing from a feminist consciousness is simply that it cannot be reabsorbed into their processions—philosophically or in terms of form. So how, precisely, does a feminist consciousness frame this movement toward the excessive [the unlawful]? Without ultimately becoming law itself?

The little Fury looks at the brother sitting between her + her mother on the verandah while the storm clouds gather. The black clouds also remind the little Fury that she is afraid. What will happen after the thunderclap explodes? Will lightning strike the house? The mother sits with her lips pursed. Earlier that day, the little Fury heard her mother crying as she scrubbed the oak floor. She understood her mother was thinking how she wanted to leave them all + be a missionary in...Africa(!)

But my heroine has paused to wonder why the little girl has become a little Fury on her computer screen. Has history finally come full circle? In the myth, the Erinyes [the Furies] hounded Oedipus to death at Colonus in Attica. His crime? Perhaps society was punishing him for unconsciously trying to substitute the matrilineal for the patrilineal line. But I like to think the Erinyes were furious at his failure. It's true that throughout history, they've always been somewhere in the picture: the witches, the suffragettes, and now the second-wave feminists. One of them, the little girl, sat on the verandah projecting herself into the mosquito [only the females bite] raising the welts on her brother's neck. Yes, *Les mouches* de Sartre. Negatively prophetic. The Erinyes, emerging again, maybe to upset the power on which the whole Oedipal drama is based, the matrilineal traces buried in the folds of classical drama. And expand them into new time, into new space hopefully opening before us as the law wavers on the edge of social, ecological disaster...

Perhaps this desire for some lost matrilineal consciousness explains the attraction of the Dark, the uncanny, for the little Erinyes sitting on the verandah, listening to the buzz of mosquitoes. There is an ominous foreboding in the black storm clouds. But a foreboding is also charged with eroticism. It occurs to my heroine looking at her computer screen that the doubleness of the little Erinyes, that bittersweet mixture of eroticism + foreboding, might hold a clue to her search for a subject who is not merely the feminine of hero: *a name given to men of superhuman strength, courage, ability, favoured by the Gods* said an old Oxford dictionary. Nor heroine as implied in the 70s wave of Anglo-American feminist criticism,[3] i.e., the female hero as logical extension of 19th-century bourgeois notions of enlightenment, where light is reason, wielded by the highest forces of moral authority to conquer 'darkness.' And by extension, also of Marxist ideology, inasmuch as the concept of total victory of light over dark was synonymous with progress. In the latter paradigm, the female hero + her kind must end up successful in their specific project, be it personal, professional, or 'revolutionary.' For there can only be the victors + the victims, the former the subjects of progressive novels.

No, my heroine imagines a new heroine closer to an earlier meaning of the word: *At Delphi a[n]... ascension ceremony conducted wholly by women was called the Herois, or "feast of the heroine."*[4] And this ascension represented Persephone's cyclical rise from Hades, not to 'heaven,' but to wander *about on the earth with Demeter (her mother) until the time came for her to return to the Underworld.*[5] It is the notion of cyclical ascension + descent (in contrast to the pattern of linear rise to climax in patriarchal drama) that appeals to my heroine as she tries to work this all out on her computer screen.

For this notion would permit her heroine [her set of heroines] to be both grandiose + humble, miserable + angry, not to mention any other imaginable contradiction, without shame...

Now, how exactly would this subject in writing be structured by her feminist consciousness? And why do I keep dancing around the issue as if to keep it at a distance?

In fiction, modernity was in part instrumental in opening the space where new subjectivities might emerge. In its desire for writing that began to dismantle subjective AUTHOR-ity. But in opening, in its new awareness of narrative-in-crisis, an evolving space for writing, a possible subject-in-the-feminine inadvertently emerged. I say inadvertently because some philosophers had taken to naming this uncoded space of writing 'feminine' [*woman is neither truth nor non-truth for Derrida + is therefore akin to the spacing which is writing*].[6] But there was resistence to the idea that this accidented space should be a site of new identitary subject formation. Your women writing cohorts, on the other hand, easily saw *identitary* subjectivity as potentially multiple. The Greeks sometimes thought of Persephone as triple: Diana in the leaves, Luna shining brightly, Persephone down below. But can this subject, like Persephone, admit to a cyclical retreat into shadow [whence Persephone was, according to the myth, at first, brutally abducted] and still be up to scratch from a feminist point of view?

It is [naturally] a grey day. My heroine is at her desk creating heroines. When, outside, suddenly appears the sun. So that the three-dimensional plane of mountain, flat-topped roofs, + the balcony look black in the shadow, with the light coming from behind like the negative of a photo. This darkish place reminds her that Walter Benjamin once said photography made MAN realize he [too] could be objectified.[7] And Barthes noted how violent was the experience of becoming that photographic object: a "micro-experience"[8] of death, he said.

Of course, the dark space in which man sees woman-the-object lurking isn't necessarily 'dark' to her. *Herself Defined,* said Barbara Guest of H.D. The latter, bolstered, one suspects, by an intimate female context that treated her as significant. Can one take off from a female-dominant space, fly out, beyond, yet still be in solidarity? Might I, despite all those mattress layers of complicity provided by feminism, admit to wanting to explore, *avant tout,* some incommensurate knot?

The sky in this narrative grows greyer. Driving down the highway with clouds banking furiously before a storm—when suddenly a terrible sense of emptiness. What does a heroine do with this? Casting about for an answer, she fastens, as the big raindrops start, on fear of an accident. Itself a projection of that almost permanent human angst of unknown source. When confronted with himself, Hamlet conjured up his father. And his [cuckolded] father said: Do something about my honour. Which Hamlet interpreted as: do something about your mother + her lover, my usurper. Does a woman, when confronted with herself, conjure her mother? Persephone had to live divided—half the year in the Underworld + half the year on Earth, where she wanted to be, with her mother.

In this, unlike Hamlet, she was not ambivalent. It was her mother who was significant.

I think Persephone's story reflects something of what draws a writer to explore the 'dark,' firing her desire to grasp the unspeakable mother in language as a being. On the verandah, something about the odd presence of her mother kept the little girl riveted. Although she didn't have the language to wonder why her mother seemed so distant [+ at the same time so penetrating]. She surveyed the welts on the neck of the brother, the mother's favourite, glad that he was allergic to mosquitoes. The fact that she was not allergic made her a superior form of being. Later, her love for Proust's writing was mixed with jealousy. He seemed to feel he had the right to expect his mother's kiss—a kiss she lacked. She wrote in her notebook:

Proust's childhood anxiety about love was based on forcing mother's kiss.

A request always to be repeated because he couldn't have it freely.

It occurred to her that a woman writing a story such as Proust's, but with a female subject, would be considered weird for wanting the kiss so much. Take Freud's Dora, whose attachment to her mother [+ to her father's mistress!] earned her the label of hysteric. Hysteric, i.e., perpetually overwrought, making a nuisance of herself. Proust's 'hysteria' resulted in a work of incredible beauty. Was he, although a gay man, still on the right side of culture? Or was it the magnificence of the writing—born in part of his 'maladjustment,' his *brisure* with what was expected of a man—that allowed for his accomplishment?

To be or not to be, for a woman, would normally involve a strong identity with the similar parent, were that parent's presence in language not often assigned a utilitarian function. Making it difficult for the little girl of [her] transitional generation to break the symbiotic hold enough to see, in the female parent, the *woman*. Who, partly obscured, often ends up in my + other prose as a semi-Gothic figure, a figure of *excess*. Also of *absence*. To be sure, feminism [her circle of women friends] has aided in the process of attributing to that figure some kind of meaning. One could think, then, that feminism would be open to exploring the shadowy side of things—given the mother's place in it. But, paradoxically, that positivism, that indomitably courageous feminist marching down a straight road toward the sun, feels more like a block when she, the writer, tries to gesture toward the negative, that inchoate space cohabited, along with the mother, by suppressed or murdered species of all kinds. At such moments feminism seems in contradiction with the poet in her, who is drawn toward *la séduction du glissement*, a fundamental function of poetic language. Where else but in poetic language may she be inscribed in all her [unnameable] complexity?

Outside my window, autumn rain beats horizontally over the stage set of façades topped with pretty, fluted decorations. I'm writing about the mother who spent her lifetime on a theological mission. She was trying to find some ultimately perfect interpretation of the Bible. Around her in the village, the Protestant sects were a mockery of her efforts; four different churches for a Protestant population of less than 300—the other 300 being French + Catholic. Naturally I was suspicious of transcendence, a suspicion that has led me to place myself, in writing, somewhere at a juncture of politics + excess. In analysis, it is thought that the most repressed parts of memory, the darkest corners, are shut doors on fascinating places. Who knows how far one must go to be freed of human nature's propensity for conventional thinking?

1973: A far-left group in Québec that claims to support the slogan All Freedom in Art. Still, I'm complaining to a comrade about what I perceive as a lack of validation of artists in the group. He says you have three strikes against you: you're English, you're a mother, you're an artist. I join forces with some surrealists, fellow travellers of the group. The key to 'total revolution,' they believed, lay in the unplumbed gold of the latent content of our dreams. We explore the unconscious through collective sessions of automatic writing. But the language did not seem to me to spring forth as unadulterated, as pure, as the others, mostly guys, thought. For one, the female figure in our language games often appeared as muse: as material for 'total revolutionaries' to use. And although I was able to access certain things that proved invaluable, the context was one in which it was difficult for me to project as gendered speaker.

Here the matter of *what's unskirtable in feminism* gains a nuance. That potentially nourishing women's circle must not only be one that fosters reinvention of the feminine, but it must be able to resist the tendency to create new convention.

The little girl tried to invent herself each day. She'd step off the curb + write in her mind: *The little girl stepped off the curb.* She'd cross the street + write in her mind: *The little girl crossed the street.* But as she grew up + started having the usual gamut of relationships, her attempts kept, given her desire to please, slipping out of focus. At the same time she felt a terrible ambivalence about that self mirrored by social expectations. It would burst forth unexpectedly, in the form of verbal attacks on the weak flanks that lovers show in intimacy. As if bearing toward the other an unabiding anger fed not by the circumstances of relationship, but by some deeper source. In horror, the young woman atoned by even more elaborate deferring. Alternately, by developing cool, offhand ways [*la belle indifférence?*] to cover her apprehension of the body *doing something inappropriate*. Reiterated in dreams. In one: across the street, the pregnant silhouette of Madame Cousineau planting her garden under a full moon. While on their verandah, her husband did a mocking two-step.

Into this narrative, feminism had come as a tremendous relief. But arriving in the warmly complicit place, she wanted more: she wanted both the legitimizing community + for that community to cast no moral judgments on her freedom to desire, to imagine. To ask so much of community was also to commit to intense engagement to it. "Your work isn't positive enough," another feminist writer told her. "It doesn't show an upbeat image of relations between women." I reply, at first feebly, then angrily, "It's about the struggle between thinking + feeling." She would ask of her community that it be adventurous enough to admit that language is meaning + play, abstraction, music, the music of the body, the material of being in + with the world.

For psychoanalysts like Jacques Lacan, it is from speech itself [la parole] that the body surges. But what if this *parole*—in speaking the imagined body—is using negative or unhelpful encoding, thus contributing to the sense of incommensurate in her? Is not the tragic moment for the classic hero—the moment he finally closes the gap between his words + acts—the moment he fails patriarchal law? For Hamlet, the point of no return was verbally acknowledging his problem: that he was a [homosexual?] traitor in terms of patriarchal values. For Oedipus, it was when he was forced to recognize that he was the very father-murderer his own words had so drastically condemned.

The more she wills herself to speak, the more absurdly alienated she finds herself in terms of the law of the Father; the gap's so great, it's almost comical. Indeed, it's here that her words start on a crazy zigzag journey, now towards the mother, now towards the culture. The spectacle of herself—, in her endlessly recomposed phrases—might have the distancing humour of a carnivalesque dance, moving toward the excess spawned by dreams, hope, memory, yet requiring the extended hand of her sisters. Who, like her, see a tremendous future in inscribing the dialectics of the subject in ways of speaking more adequate for her pluralistic spectacle. Like Virginia Woolf, she's bored with narrative:

> *Also, why not invent a new kind of play:*
> *Woman thinks...*
> *He does.*
> *Organ plays.*
> *She writes.*
> *They say:*
> *She sings.*
> *Night speaks.*
> *They miss.*9

She looks out the window, at the harsh post-rain light topping the pediments opposite, thinking she has the right setting for her heroine(s). The cloud-piercing ray glazing the pediments is, in its relationship to the quickly falling night, rather like the image she projects on her women's circle: a lit-up space, *glee* slanting off what might be otherwise perceived as shadow; glittering with the whole weight of night around it. As in a carnival, where resonate polyphonic voices, people of any walk or privilege. She is there with her sisters, amid the carnival's blizzard of anecdotes—but no narrative, no moralizing boundaries. All of these things, she thinks, mirror her own ambivalence. Confession [as per Hamlet or Oedipus] is pointless, is closure. We can only distance from that old containment of us [we can't erase the body's 'inappropriateness']. The dissolution of subjects into the frenzy of the carnival, each, recomposing again, again. She + her sisters, dressed for the explosion, parading in the gap between desire + the residue of experience, between ideology + unconsciousness, between the mask [a slant attempt at synthesis of meaning] + the laughter that in the same breath assures transgression.

She knows this tragicomic act is not the only fictional performance possible on this stage/street. It is not the only way of indicating the widening gap between herself + History's dramas. What is unskirtable about her feminism is what structures the cognizant of now. There are other fictions, other theories, other utopias. Other moments. But now, she the feminist, she the artist, is in her third-floor apartment getting dressed in her robes of ambivalence, in her mask, which is her comment on her current grasp of meaning. To go + join the carnival below.

Montréal, 1988
Revised, 2013, 2020

AFTERWORD

by Margaret Christakos

Gail Scott recognizes the shape of her sentences as they are coming into change—as contradictory as this sounds, it is key to conversing with all of her compositional impulses. At the threshold of reissuing selected essays on writing from the 1970s and 1980s, with a brilliant suite of new and revised essays that run contemporaneously with her novels from the mid-'90s through to the present moment, Gail Scott's capacity to continually reinstigate writing-as-change is delightfully audible.

Resisting any tactic to explain or historicize the older essays, all of these essays exist as aesthetic experiments of their own. Assembling the manuscript involved the polyphonic archive: Gail drew together articles, talks prepared for readings and colloquia, interviews, literary journal contributions, notebook texts about practice and bearing, and critical writings, and worked with their multiple vectors as moving parts.

As such, the book contains two juicy lobes. First, an interlinking suite of Gail's newly composed and revised essays instigated over the last two decades, under the beguiling queer title "The Smell of Fish." These are paired, as to a second lobe, with selections from her stunning collection of essays on feminist writing from *Spaces Like Stairs* (1989), newly selected and revised here.

Titling is hard. I suggested possibilities drawn from her own metaphors: *A Prose Is a Prose Is a Prose. Unsaid in the Cusps of Meaning. Sentenced to Explode. Words Sitting Differently. Never Pretending Whole. Radical Unclosure.* Gail conveyed it with *Permanent Revolution*: the never-settled mutual orbits of art and social transformation—all of it at risk of flying apart, intent on "the artist's fundamental task: to be a critic of her entire moment, with all its contradicting vectors."

These essays direct their pull to other writers and thinkers thinking through a radical poetics meaningful for social change. Gail Scott's experimental prose signals in the ongoing present like this, each essay caressing in some sense the others, dispersing an elixir spiked with excess and bold exactitude. These essays never swerve from reconnoitring with the queer and political: that a writer needs to cause permanent revolution in the world, to language, to genre, to make leakier shapes of identity, gender, and narrative.

Margaret Christakos
Toronto, 2021

NOTES

PREFACE

1. *Permanent Revolution* is the title of a work by anti-Stalinist Leon Trotsky.

EXCESS + THE FEMININE

1. Majorie Welish, *Isle of the Signatories* (Minneapolis: Coffee House Press, 2008).
2. Édouard Glissant, in *Les entretiens Bâton Rouge: Avec Alexandre Leupin* (Paris: Gallimard, 2008).
3. Leonora Carrington, "Down Below" in *The House of Fear* (New York: E. P. Dutton, 1988).
4. Gail Scott, *Heroine* (Toronto: Coach House Books, 2019).
5. Judith Butler, "The Body You Want" [Interview with Liz Kotz], *Artforum* 31:3 (November 1992).

5. Jacques Roubaud, *La fleur inverse* (Paris: Éditions Ramsay, 1986).

6. Viktor Shklovsky, "Art as Technique" in *The Critical Tradition: Classic Texts and Contemporary Trends*, comp. David H. Richter, 3rd ed. (Bedford St. Martin's/Macmillan 2017).

7. Liz Howard, "Of Hereafter Song," *The Capilano Review* 3.16 (Winter 2012): Ecologies.

8. Lisa Robertson, *Nilling* (Toronto: Book*hug Press, 2012).

9. Jane Bowles, in *Collected Writings*, ed. Millicent Dillon (New York: New American Library, 2017).

10. Renee Gladman, *The Activist* (San Francisco: Krupskaya, 2003).

THE ATTACK OF DIFFICULT WOMEN PROSE

1. Lynne Tillman, "Everything Is Nice," electricliterature. com (2013).

2. Jacques Derrida, speaking of Marx, in *Specters of Marx, The State of the Debt, The Work of Mourning, & The New International*, trans. Peggy Kamuf (Abingdon, UK: Routledge, 1994).

3. Carla Harryman, *Adorno's Noise* (Buffalo: Essay Press, 2008).

4. Eileen Myles, *The Importance of Being Iceland: Travel Essays in Art* (New York: Semiotext(e), 2009).

5. Harryman, *Adorno's Noise*.

6. Viktor Shklovsky, *Zoo*, trans. Richard Sheldon (Normal, IL: Dalkey Archive Press, 2001).

7. CA Conrad, *While Standing in Line for Death* (New York: Wave Books, 2017).

8. Derrida citing Karl Marx, *Specters of Marx*.

9. Eileen Myles, *Evolution* (New York: Grove Press, 2019).
10. Samuel Beckett, "Play" in *The Collected Shorter Plays* (New York: Grove Press, 2010).
11. Juliet Stevenson "Interview," *Independent* (January 2014).
12. Charles Bernstein/Marjorie Perloff, in "A Conversation with Charles Bernstein," writing.upenn.edu/epc/authors/perloff/articles/mp_cb.html.
13. Rod Smith, cited by Juliana Spahr and David Buuck in *An Army of Lovers* (San Francisco: City Lights, 2013).

SOFT THINGS, HARD THINGS

1. Carla Harryman in *From Our Hearts to* Yours, ed. Rob Halpern and Robin Tremblay-McGaw (Oakland, CA: On Contemporary Practice, 2017).
2. The Vancouver New Poetics Colloquium, 1985: In fact, the so-called dominant males [Rob Silliman, Bruce Andrews + others] caught my attention at this conference organized by the excellent Kootenay School of Writing; Looking back, I see the list of interveners was well provided with women poets [Lyn Hejinian, Susan Howe, Daphne Marlatt + others].
3. Robert Glück, "Long Note on New Narrative" in *Biting the Error: Writers Explore Narrative*, ed. Robert Glück, Gail Scott, et al. (Toronto: Coach House Books, 2004), 27.
4. *A Little Girl Dreams of Taking the Veil*, performed at the Arts, San Francisco, January 1995. Music by Erling Wold, libretto by Max Ernst, dramaturgy by Carla Harryman, directed by Jim Cave.
5. Glück, "Long Note," 30.
6. Laure, *Écrits* (Paris: Union Générale d'Éditions, 1978).

7. Ibid.

8. Ibid.

9. Ibid.

10. Roland Barthes, *Writing Degree Zero* (London: Hill and Wang, 1977), re-issue.

11. Monique Wittig, in *The Straight Mind and Other Essays* (Boston: Beacon, 1992).

12. Hubert Aquin, *Next Episode*, trans. Sheila Fischman (Toronto: McClelland & Stewart, 2001).

CORPUS DELICTI

1. Nathanaël, *Hatred of Capitalism* (New York: Nightboat, 2019). In the original citation, 'foreign' is footnoted by Nathanaël, who explains: *I insist on this particular archaism, the reinforcement of dividing lines that inevitably confound themselves in the mixage of bodies....*

2. Édouard Glissant, in *Les entretiens Bâton Rouge: Avec Alexandre Leupin* (Paris: Gallimard, 2008) [trans. Gail Scott].

3. James Baldwin, speaking in Berkeley, CA, 1979.

4. Jean Daive, *Sous la coupole* (Paris: Éditions POL, 1996).

5. Jean Daive, *Under the Dome: Walks with Paul Celan*, trans. Rosmarie Waldrop (San Francisco: City Lights, 2020).

6. Ibid.

7. Ibid.

8. Gail Scott, "How to Be a Fellow Traveller," in *Arc Poetry Magazine* 84 (2017).

THE SUTURED SUBJECT

1. Rita Wong, *Forage* (Vancouver: Nightwood Editions, 2007).

2. Friedrich A. Kittler, *Gramophone, Film, Typewriter* (Stanford, CA: University of Stanford Press, 1999).

3. Fred Moten, in *Black and Blur* (Durham, NC: Duke University Press, 2017).

4. Gail Scott, *The Obituary* (Toronto: Coach House Books, 2010; New York: Nightboat, 2012).

5. Mina Loy, *The Last Lunar Baedeker* (New York: Farrar, Straus and Giroux, 1997), reprint edition.

6. Robert Glück, "Long Note on New Narrative" in *Biting the Error: Writers Explore Narrative*, ed. Robert Glück, Gail Scott et al. (Toronto: Coach House Books, 2004), 26.

7. Kim Rosenfield & Gail Scott, "Gail Scott: Broken and Accidental Topographies in *The Obituary*" [Interview], *Bomb Magazine* (September 2013).

8. Tricia Low, *Socialist Realism* (Minneapolis: Coffee House Press, 2019).

9. Meredith Quartermain & Gail Scott, "Interview," *The Capilano Review* 3.41 (Summer 2020).

10. Dodie Bellamy & Kevin Killian, eds., *Writers Who Love Too Much* (New York: Nightboat, 2017).

11. Renee Gladman, "The Person in the World," in *Biting the Error*, 47.

12. Kathy Acker, "The Killers," in *Biting the Error*, 17.

13. Antonin Artaud, *Collected Works, Volume 1*, trans. Victor Corti (Parchment, MI: Riverrun Press, 1999).

14. Rosenfield & Scott, *Bomb Magazine*.

15. Robert Glück, in *Denny Smith* (Astoria, OR: Clear Cut Press, 2003).

16. Wong, *Forage*.

THE POROUS TEXT

1. Gail Scott, *My Paris* (Toronto: Mercury Press; Chicago: Dalkey Archive, 2003).
2. Raymond Chandler, *The Long Goodbye* (New York: Vintage Crime, 1988).
3. Barrett Watten, *The Constructivist Moment* (Middletown, CT: Wesleyan University Press, 2003).
4. Gertrude Stein, "Plays," in *Lectures in America* (New York: Random House, 1935).
5. Gail Scott, *Heroine* (Toronto: Coach House Books, 2019).
6. Walter Benjamin, *The Arcades Project* (Cambridge, MA: Harvard University Press: 2002).
7. Ibid.
8. Scott, *My Paris*.
9. Douglas A. Martin, from "22 Points" [unpublished essay].

INTRODUCTION 2020

1. The group was comprised of Nicole Brossard, Louky Bersianik, Louise Dupré, Louise Cotnoir, France Théoret, and myself.

VIRGINIA AND COLETTE

1. Colette, *Earthly Paradise* (selected extracts), ed. Robert Phelps (Harmondsworth, Middlesex: Penguin, 1974).
2. Luce Irigaray, *Ce sexe qui n'en est pas un* (Paris: Les Editions de Minuit, 1977).
3. Colette, *Earthly Paradise*: 132.
4. Claude Beausoleil, unedited text, March 1981.

5. Nicole Brossard, *Le centre blanc* (Montréal: Les Éditions d'Orphée, 1970). My reading here of this piece is coloured by readings of later Brossard work. It was in about 1973 that Brossard started insisting on the specifically feminine in the act of writing.

6. Hélène Cixous, "The Laugh of the Medusa," trans. Keith Cohen & Paula Cohen, in *New French Feminisms*, ed. Elaine Marks & Isabelle de Courtivron (New York: Schocken, 1981).

7. Michel Tremblay, *Thérèse et Pierrette a l'école des Saints-Anges* (Montréal: Leméac, 1980).

8. Author's insertion, added 1988. Jespersen's *Growth and Structure of the English Language* (Chicago: Chicago University Press, 1982), can be read as the historical account of the growing sharpening and efficacy of English, at the expense, in part, of the feminine, until grammar, lexicon, and "words and turns that are found, and words and turns that are not found" combine to give English its masculine clarity.

9. Philippe Sollers, *Vision à New York* (Paris: Grasset, 1981).

10. France Théoret, *Nous parlerons comme on écrit* (Montréal: Les Herbes Rouges, 1982).

11. This essay was also anthologized in *A Mazing Space: Writing Canadian Women Writing*, ed. Shirley Neuman and Smaro Kamboureli (Edmonton: Longspoon/Newest, 1986).

A VISIT TO CANADA

1. Roland Barthes distinguishes between the readerly text, the text which provides reader pleasure but does not challenge the reader subject position, who thus maintains a

passive posture vis-à-vis the text; + the writerly text, which provides an intense relationship of *bliss* between writer + reader, by virtue of constantly challenging the reader to do the active work of questioning codes, of breaking out of her subject position.

2. Roland Barthes, *Roland Barthes by Roland Barthes*, trans. Richard Howard (New York: Hill and Wang, 1977).
3. Luce Irigaray, notably in *Ce sexe qui n'en est pas un* (Paris: Les Editions de Minuit, 1977).
4. Nicole Brossard, "L'écrivain," *La nef des sorcières* (Montréal: Les Editions Quinze, 1976: 74-75) [trans. Gail Scott].
5. Louky Bersianik, *Les agénésies du vieux monde* (Montréal: L'Intégrale Editrice, 1982) [trans. Gail Scott].

A STORY BETWEEN TWO CHAIRS

1. This essay was published in French in *la nouvelle barre du jour* 141 (1984).

PARAGRAPHS BLOWING ON A LINE

1. Roland Barthes, *The Pleasure of the Text* (New York: Hill and Wang, 1975).
2. Carla Harryman, *The Middle* (San Francisco: Gaz, 1983).
3. Barthes, *Pleasure of the Text*.

A FEMINIST AT THE CARNIVAL

1. Revised and co-published in Gail Scott et al., *Theory, A Sunday* (New York: Belladonna, 2013), + *La théorie, un dimanche* (Montréal: les éditions du remue-ménage, 1988, 2019).

2. Nicole Brossard (spoken at an organizing meeting of the International Feminist Book Fair, October 1988).

3. I am thinking of the kind of criticism that often appeared in militant feminist periodicals of the 70s + early 80s, where books were judged politically 'correct' according to certain criteria: a woman must be 'strong' not a 'victim' etc., although exactly what was meant by those terms varied greatly according to the critic.

4. Robert Graves, *Greek Myths* (London: Cassell, 1965).

5. Ibid.

6. From Alice Jardine's reading of Jacques Derrida's *Spurs: Nietzsche's Styles*, in ch. 9 of *Gynesis* (Ithaca, NY: Cornell University Press, 1986).

7. Walter Benjamin, "La photographie," in *Poésie et révolution* (Paris: Denoël, 1971).

8. Roland Barthes, *La chambre claire* (Paris: Editions du Seuil, 1980).

9. Virginia Woolf, *A Writer's Diary* (New York: Harcourt Brace Jovanovich, 1953).

ACKNOWLEDGEMENTS

Thanks to Jay MillAr and Hazel Millar for tremendous work as publishers of Book*hug Press, and for an open, sensitive approach to the subject of editing.

Thanks to Margaret Christakos for her wisdom and brilliance, and for patience! This book would be so much less without Margaret's perspicacious editing.

There are so many writers to whom I am indebted, over time, for stimulating conversation, invaluable friendship, + incredible writing. To name a very few: France Théoret, Nicole Brossard, the late Louky Bersianik, Louise Bouchard, Louise Cotnoir, Louise Dupré, Fred Wah, Liz Howard, Zoe Whittall, Nathanaël, Rachel Zolf, Margaret Christakos, Nicole Markotic, Armand Ruffo, Lisa Robertson, Sabrina Soyer, Eileen Myles, Marjorie Welish, Carla

Harryman, Renee Gladman, Brenda Coultas, John Keene, Stacy Szymaszek, Tisa Bryant, Robert Glück, Rachel Levitsky, Kim Rosenfield, Yedda Morrison, Camille Roy, Dodie Bellamy, the late great Kevin Killian, Chris Kraus, Charles Bernstein, Barrett Watten, Robbie Schwartzwald, WM Burton, Daniel Scott, Andy Fitch, Jane Malcolm.

I owe a very special thanks to Kim Rosenfield for the brilliance of her *Bomb* interview as cited in "The Sutured Subject" essay. It opened for me more articulate ways to think about my writing, especially with respect to *The Obituary*.

Several essays in "The Smell of Fish" section contain revisited short excerpts of texts + interviews previously published in, among others, *Matrix, The Ottawa Poetry Newsletter, Quebec Studies, Tripwire, Jacket 2, Brick, Arc Poetry Magazine, Review of Contemporary Fiction, Bomb Magazine, Rain Taxi, Chain, Spirale, Lettres Québécoises, The Capilano Review, The Poetry Project Newsletter*, among many others. In addition, essays or earlier versions of the selected essays in the "Spaces Like Stairs" section appeared in *Room of One's Own (Tessera), Canadian Fiction Magazine (Tessera), Trivia, Canadian Forum*, + *la nouvelle barre du jour*. Sincere thanks to the editors of these literary journals who so often play a seminal role in the writing world.

A special thanks to Michel Vrana for a fabulous cover + inside page design.

Thanks to Stuart Ross for meticulous proofreading.

And always to my daughter Anna for support, love, and friendship.

ABOUT THE AUTHOR

GAIL SCOTT is the author of *Spare Parts* (1981), *Heroine* (1987, re-issued in 2019 with an introduction by Eileen Myles), *Main Brides* (1993), *My Paris* (1999/2003), *Spare Parts Plus Two* (2002), and *The Obituary* (2010/2012), finalist for *Le Grand Prix du Livre de la Ville de Montréal*. Her essays are collected in *Spaces Like Stairs* (1989) and in *La Théorie, un dimanche* (1988) which was translated into English as *Theory, A Sunday* (2013). Scott is co-editor of the New Narrative anthology *Biting the Error: Writers Explore Narrative* (2004). Her translation of Michael Delisle's *Le désarroi du matelot* was shortlisted for a 2001 Governor General's Literary Award. A memoir, based in Lower Manhattan during the early Obama years, is forthcoming. Scott lives in Montréal.

Manufactured as the first edition of
Permanent Revolution
in the spring of 2021 by Book*hug Press

Edited for the press by Margaret Christakos
Copy edited by Stuart Ross
Type + design by Michel Vrana

bookhugpress.ca